HEAD
OVER
HEELS

HEAD OVER HEELS

Gymnastics for Children

VERA L. DREHMAN

❋

Illustrations by
ALENE HOLDAHL

Harper & Row
NEW YORK, EVANSTON, AND LONDON

WITH FOND MEMORIES OF AND DEEPEST GRATITUDE to

The American Sokol Organization

AND

TO THE MEN AND WOMEN WHO SHARE SO MUCH
OF THEMSELVES WITH OUR CHILDREN BY GIVING
FREELY OF THEIR TIME AND SKILLS THROUGH

The YMCA and YWCA
Boys' Clubs of America
City Recreation Departments
The Schools
The YMHA and YWHA

CONTENTS

❁

INTRODUCTION

❁

Head over Heels presents a new approach to a family of
familiar sports—gymnastics, tumbling, marching maneuvers,
and track. Its instruction methods are tailored to the child,
with careful allowance made for the needs or limitations of
children of different age levels, interests, and aptitudes.
Special attention is given to adjusting equipment and to the
techniques of precautionary guarding known as "spotting."

The guiding principle in the procedures outlined is that of
systematic progression. For each of the various sports broad
coverage is given to the basics which develop strength, coordination, and timing. By spending a generous amount
of time in developing such fundamentals, one creates a wide
margin for safety and establishes a sound base for further
learning. Exercises on the elementary and intermediate levels
have been presented in separate sections. Careful evaluation
has been made of building programs suitable for boys and for
girls. Activities for boys emphasize strength, timing, and the
development of muscle tone in the upper torso. Those for girls
stress timing, grace, poise, and the toning of muscles, par-
ticularly those of the abdomen.

The pertinence of gymnastics for today's children becomes
apparent when we consider the amount of time they spend
riding in cars and watching television. Vigorous physical
exercise, regularly performed and combined with the self-
discipline required by gymnastics, offers one of the finest ways
to build strong bodies and healthy minds. Gymnastics also

offers another value, somewhat less obvious but no less important. Competition with oneself is inherent in all apparatus work, tumbling, and track events. Each day the performer hopes to do better than he did the day before. When he succeeds, it gives him a deep sense of accomplishment. The fact that Jimmy does it still better becomes of minor importance. The contest is with himself.

Since mastery and sharpening skill are the child's own rewards of self-discipline, the instructor should, in all fairness to the child, stress total effort—always keeping in mind, of course, individual limitations or capabilities. Although it will not be possible for all students to perform all the activities described in this manual, each can experience a feeling of success and most can become adept in some aspects of the program. It is hoped that this book will bring to many children the opportunity to enjoy to the full the benefits of that wonderful sport gymnastics and its relatives—tumbling, track events, and marching maneuvers.

HEAD
OVER
HEELS

1

❀ ❀ ❀

SAFETY
MEASURES

Common sense is the best safety measure to apply in any sport. There are, however, certain procedures which should be established and which can mean the difference between a high accident rate and a low one.

Always check the gym floor or activity area for any item that could cause a fall. Make a regular check for holes in the mats and give careful scrutiny to the condition of the rope. Require that students' clothing shall be close-fitting so it cannot catch on the apparatus. In order to prevent slipping, students should wear sneakers, or the ballet-type slippers that some girls prefer.

Since each type of activity presents its own special situations, safety measures for the various sports are considered separately.

Tumbling

Wide mats must be used for the learner in tumbling. A safety belt, described on page 16, should be used, as indicated, for certain exercises.

Games

When young children play games usually played with a volleyball, substitute a medium-sized plastic ball.

Track Events

The use of mats for the hurdles is highly advisable. Use one mat in front of the high jump and two or three behind it.

Apparatus Activities

To avoid having to adjust the apparatus for each child, the class may be divided into teams according to height. After the apparatus is set up, each piece well separated from the others, assign a team to each piece of equipment. When all members of each team have performed, the teams should rotate, each team moving to the next piece of equipment.

Orderly conduct during apparatus-activity time is essential. The pupils at each piece of equipment should remain in line, in the at-ease stance (figure on p. 45). The line should be formed well away from the apparatus and off the mats. It is important that the children do not wander about. Distraction can cause a performer to falter and fall.

Systematic progression is the cardinal safety rule in gymnastic activities involving apparatus. Slow progression from the simple to the difficult insures sufficient strength, timing, and coordination for the child to advance to the next more difficult stunt. Remember that muscle fatigue can strike suddenly without warning. Each exercise should be learned and practiced thoroughly before going on to a new one.

Observe the following rules in apparatus work:

Use mats under all apparatus.

Never allow a chair or any other object to be left under the apparatus.

Do not allow gum chewing. Gum can easily become lodged in the windpipe while a simple somersault or upstart movement is being performed.

4

Require students to remove all jewelry before gym class begins.

Eyeglasses should be removed, but may be replaced after the exercise is completed if vision so requires.

Discourage laughing while a performer is on the apparatus. A performer's laugh may loosen his grip and result in a fall.

Require the use of safety belts where so indicated in this manual, until skill and confidence are acquired.

Have chalk available to be used on the hands when they become moist. It can be purchased at drugstores in cake form.

PRELIMINARY CONDITIONING OF MUSCLES

If the student is introduced to both mat and apparatus work at the same time and he progresses in both areas in the order outlined in the exercises, the necessary strength for each successive stunt should be developed. When such progression has not been followed, however, preliminary conditioning calisthenics are in order.

The Arms

Push-ups are good arm strengtheners and should precede any straight-arm supports on the parallel bars. A drop between the bars can be very painful.

The Spine

The spine-stretching movements in the chapter "Tumbling and Free Exercise" should be worked into gradually. There should be no straining. It takes time to work out the "bugs" in stiff spines and to stretch the muscles of the rear thigh.

The Knees

Incorporate knee exercises into the conditioning calisthenics. The knees absorb the shock of dismounts from the apparatus. This is a natural function of the knees, however, and children have little difficulty, if reminded, to bend the knees as they land on the mat, leading with the toes.

The Ankles

The correct manner of landing should become a habit. The drop to the mat should be executed with the toes leading, followed by a landing on the balls of the feet. The knees should be bent as the landing is made. The landing should be started about twelve inches above the mat. If this procedure is not followed, the child may experience a needle-prick pain in the ankles. The feet must always be together on landing.

The Neck

The simple forward roll should be preceded by education of the neck muscles. Many children have been injured by dropping from the squat position onto the neck because they have neglected to tuck the head onto the chest and use the arms as support.

It is wise to start the first few rolls with the top of the head on the mat. This puts the child in the position of having to bear the weight of his body on the head and neck, and results in conscious awareness of the need to brace the neck area. An infant goes through this same process in his experimentation with body movement. After several experiences with the head-first roll, the standard forward roll may be safely introduced.

BUMPS AND BRUISES

Bruises sometimes appear which are not easily traceable to bumps or falls. These usually appear (1) on the underside of the upper arm, (2) just below the elbow, or (3) on the pelvic bones on either side of the abdomen. On the upper arm and forearm the bruises may appear because there is not enough muscle to tense against the pressure. The upper-arm hang and forearm support on the parallel bars may produce such bruises on a young child. After the muscles develop sufficiently, the bruises should not appear if the child performs on

6

bars which can be narrowed to the width of his shoulders. The need for quality apparatus is evident. The bruises on the front of the pelvis are often due to improper positioning of the body on the uneven parallel bars.

2

❋ ❋ ❋

SPOTTING TECHNIQUES

The term "spotting" refers to the precautionary methods used to guard the performer from injury or to give the learner added confidence. Spotters are stationed near the performer in certain tumbling acts and at all pieces of apparatus.

While based on the same principles as spotting techniques used for adults, those used for children include certain added precautionary measures. One of the significant differences is found in the use of the hand-on-hand spotting grip in introducing the child to the apparatus. This not only gives the child added confidence but can provide instant warning to the spotter. A tremble of the child's hand may be a warning of muscle fatigue and loosening grip. Stunts executed in a hanging position should be spotted with one hand on the hand or on the upper arm, the other in the area of the mid-torso—front or back, as needed. The purpose of the torso guard is to keep one hand between the performer and the mat. The guarding hand moves with the performer while the other hand stabilizes the grip on the apparatus. Remember that hand-on-hand spotting for introducing young children to

Hand-on-Hand Spotting Grip

Upper-Arm and Torso Spotting

apparatus work is insufficient in itself. It should always be used *with* the torso guard. For older children who have more weight and better muscle control, the spotter should place one hand on the upper arm, and use the other for the torso guard.

SPOTTING THE
FORWARD-SWING DISMOUNT

The forward-swing dismount requires special spotting techniques. It is the tendency of the novice to continue the legs upward instead of arching the back and leading downward with his legs. Such upward leg movement may cause him to fall on the back of his head. To watch for this, the spotter should focus his attention on the back of the performer's shoulders, as a forward-swing dismount is made.

The first apparatus activity in which the performer learns to use the forward-swing dismount is the simple forward underswing on the low horizontal bar. Here he can learn proper execution of the dismount while the factor of height is negligible. The spotter for the beginner should squat or kneel, depending on the height of the bar. He then places one hand on the child's hand or arm; and, just as the body passes under the bar, extends his free arm under the performer's shoulders, following body motion until the dismount is completed. The spotter should use his strongest arm (see

9

figure A, below) for guarding the shoulders. Should the legs be thrust up rather than down, the spotter should bring his guarding arm up, thus breaking the backward rotation (see

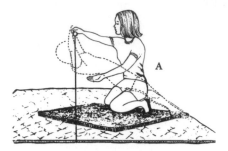

Spotting Forward-Swing Dismount

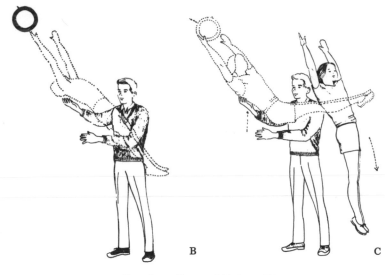

Spotting Forward-Swing Dismount from Flying Rings

figure B, above) and preventing head or shoulders from hitting the mat first. The performer will feel no ill effects if he lands on his buttocks. This technique is not hard on the spotter because the distance between the bar and the mat is not great.

In spotting the forward-swing dismount from the flying rings, the spotter must stand, arms ready, at the point where the forward swing will reach its greatest height. Here the extended-arm guard is more critical and requires a strong upward thrust. For the still rings, it may be necessary to hold the performer's arm on the first attempt at dismount. From the parallel bars, the forward-swing dismount should not require the shoulder guard, as one hand of the performer maintains a grip on the near bar until dismount is completed.

SPOTTING OTHER APPARATUS ACTIVITIES

Side Horse

The side horse is spotted from the front and side. This is where the student will land. As the hands of the performer are placed on the pommels (handles), the spotter should grasp the arm closest to him in two places—above the wrist and on the upper arm. This grip is retained until the landing is completed. Certain exceptions are mentioned in specific exercises outlined later.

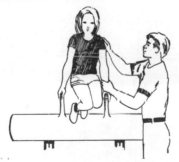

Spotting Side Horse Activities

Parallel Bars

For the parallel bars, spotting is always from the side. Stunts performed below the bars are spotted with one hand on the upper arm, the other guarding the torso from the mat, ready to break a fall. Hand-on-hand spotting may be used with younger children when it is combined with the torso guard. The torso may be guarded from above or below the bars, depending on the height of the bars. Hand-guarding the torso is important in preventing overbalancing forward or backward.

Stunts above the parallel bars are guarded with one hand on the forearm, the other on the upper arm or on the back or legs. If floor or ring exercises have accompanied or preceded the work on parallel bars, arms should have developed sufficient strength to avoid the problem of muscle fatigue.

Spotting Technique for Rings

Spotting Technique for
Beginners

The Rings

When rings are shoulder height or lower, the motions are similar to those performed below the parallel bars, and are spotted similarly. Swings executed from still rings at chin height are guarded at the waist and from the side.

The spotter stands to one side and slightly back of the performer, except for chin-ups, where it is easier to spot from behind the performer. When children perform on the rings the spotter's attention should be focused on the torso area. Trying to catch flying arms or legs is futile. As the upstart movement is made with a kick-off from the mat, rings at shoulder height, it is best to place one hand on the arm of the performer and the other on his leading leg (see figure A, p. 12) then spot the back as the legs pass above the torso (see figure B, p. 12).

Low Horizontal Bar

For the low horizontal bar, spotting is from the side or from the back and side of the apparatus. The initial hand-on-hand spotting, combined with the torso guard, is followed by arm-torso grips. One hand must be between the performer and the mat at all times.

In spotting rotation on the horizontal bar, the spotter should be on the side toward which the body rotates—except in the instance of full circles, when he should be on the side where the circle will be completed. By positioning himself on the side toward which the body will rotate in partial revolutions, he can provide full protection as the student nears the mat, lands, and recovers. In the case of attempted full circle, the spotter stationed on the side where the circle is expected to be completed can prevent return rotation if momentum is insufficient to complete a full circle. In such an event, the spotter holds his arm out, palm up, as the three-quarters mark in the circle is passed. This is to help steady or catch the body at this point. He should make no effort to touch the performer at this time, unless necessary.

Balance Beam for Girls

The first walks, dips, and turns on the balance beam for girls are assisted from the side, the spotter holding one hand. Scales may require more support, in which case the grasp is on the hand and the upper arm. More advanced students on the high beam are generally spotted on the opposite side from the one on which the performer mounts. Until good balance is developed on the low beam, work on the high beam should not be attempted, since this is difficult to spot.

SPOTTING TRACK EVENTS

High Jump

Here the spotter is largely a bystander, his duty being to adjust the rod and make certain the rod is on the side *opposite* from the origin of the jump.

Broad Jump

The spotter for the broad jump sees to it that an accurate record of jumps is kept. In the indoor broad jump the spotter makes sure that the beatboard and mats are in place. They need adjustment from time to time. In the outdoor jumping pit, the sand must be smoothed over and evened after each jump to afford proper padding.

Low Hurdles

The spotter should check the course for foreign objects and be sure the hurdle is placed on a flat surface so that it topples readily.

3

❀ ❀ ❀

TUMBLING
AND FREE
EXERCISE

Children can become reasonably adept at the basic building blocks of tumbling. The stunts are challenging, yet there are few children who find them too difficult to master. Mats or a thick lawn, and a safety belt for the more advanced students, are the only items of equipment needed. The pleasures and benefits of this phase of gymnastics are, therefore, open to all.

Free exercise combines the best parts of tumbling, ballet, and ballet warm-up stretches, with some purely imaginative movements which freely express the performer's individual approach. In Olympic competition, women's free exercise is performed to musical accompaniment of the performer's choice. The male performers work in silence. All routines are based on balance and flexibility; but men's routines emphasize a show of strength, while the women's routines place the emphasis on grace and poise.

Free exercise is one of the most dramatic and satisfying aspects of gymnastics. It demonstrates movements developed through apparatus work, but the free-exercise performer is without mechanical equipment and must, therefore, depend entirely upon his own skills.

The exercises in this chapter are designed to lay a firm foundation for any of a thousand or more routines based on the basic movement—possible variations are as numerous as the mind is fertile. As imagination devises new and exciting stunts, acquired skill makes performance a joy. This dual challenge to body and mind is recognized as one of the most fascinating aspects of gymnastics.

Safety Belts

To make a safety belt to be used in tumbling or free exercise, double a length of strong rope. Place the rope around the waist of the performer and twist the rope at both ends to form a comfortably fitting belt. A spotter is stationed at each end of the rope. The spotters should move forward or backward, or remain standing, depending on the activity of the performer, always keeping the rope high enough to prevent the performer's head from touching the mat.

Rope Safety Belt

Towel Safety Belt

Two good-sized towels may be used instead of the rope. Place one towel in front of the performer and one in back of him. Twist the ends of the towels until they fit comfortably around the waist of the performer and use as above.

ELEMENTARY TUMBLING AND FREE EXERCISE

CROSS-LEG GET-UP

Start: Standing position.
1. Cross legs at ankles; fold arms across chest.
2. Descend slowly to a sit on mat.
3. With legs and arms still crossed, tuck feet closely under body and rise slowly to standing position, weight on outer sides of feet.

Finish: Erect stand, arms at sides.

Cross-Leg Get-Up

SQUAT-TO-TOE TOUCH

Start: Squat.
1. Rest hands on floor in front of feet, palms down.
2. Rise slowly, fingers touching toes, until legs are straight.
3. Hold for several seconds.

Finish: Straighten into stand, arms at sides, good posture.

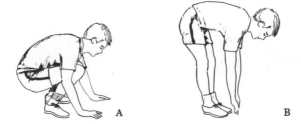

A   B

Squat-to-Toe Touch

Many children are not able to bend the spine to this extent. They should hold the extreme limit of bend which does not involve excessive strain. Flexibility of spine will come with practice.

SQUAT-TO-FLOOR TOUCH

Start: Squat.
1. Rest hands on floor in front of feet.
2. Without moving the hands, rise slowly until legs are straight.

Finish: Erect stand, arms at sides.

Toe touches are good warm-up exercises.

Squat-to-Floor Touch

LEAP FROG

Start: Two children stand side by side.
1. One child kneels and bends into low or straight-arm squat; second child steps behind him.
2. Second child places arms on squatter's back and leaps over him, legs straight, toes pointed.
3. Action is repeated, children alternating from leaping to squatting, to end of mat.

A   B

Leap Frog

Finish: Stand, side by side.

Relay races may be based on this stunt. Always use a mat or a lawn area.

SEAL WALK

Start: Kneeling position, arms on mat and forward of knees.
1. Begin to "walk" on arms, keeping legs straight up, thus causing body to stretch out.
2. Continue to walk on arms, dragging legs held straight, toes pointed.
3. Continue to end of mat.

Finish: Rise to stand.

A rocking motion occurs, hence the name "seal walk."

Seal Walk

HEEL SLAP

Start: Stand, arms at sides.
1. Make a strong jump upward, knees bent.
2. With the hands, slap heels from the side.
3. Land.
4. Repeat several times.

Finish: Stand, arms at sides.

Goal should be at least ten heel slaps in succession.

Heel Slap

Start: Two children—one kneels with hands on mat forward
of knees; the other child stands behind the first.

1. Standing child bends and grasps partner's feet at instep.
2. He returns to standing position, raising partner's legs until
they are parallel to floor.
3. Both sections of wheelbarrow move forward, one walking
on hands, with legs held rigid; the other walking and supporting partner's legs.

Wheelbarrow

Finish: Return to stand.

A relay race may be based on this stunt. Because young
arms often give way, always have this stunt performed on a
mat or a thick lawn.

HORIZONTAL SPINE STRETCH

Start: Lying position, arms at sides, palms down.

1. Raise legs slowly, keeping knees rigid, toes pointed.
2. Keeping the legs together, rotate the legs backward as hips
flex and buttocks rise off mat.
3. Keeping the arms flat on mat, palms down, pass the legs
over the chest, ending with toes touching the mat behind
the head.
4. Hold.
5. Reverse action, on slow, deliberate fashion.

Finish: Lying position.

Variation: After hold, bend knees; bring arms up over head and between the legs; grasp ankles.

Return should be slow. Eventually control should develop to a point where the back can be lowered, vertebra by vertebra. The very young lack patience with the slowness. Older girls, in particular, should be encouraged to practice the slow descent.

Horizontal Spine Stretch

SITTING SPINE-AND-LEG STRETCH

Start: Either sitting or lying position.

1. Bring arms and body forward, bending back as much as possible without undue strain. Keep legs straight, toes pointed.
2. Stretch arms forward and grasp shins or ankles, according to agility.
3. Lower head to legs, bending elbows at the same time.
4. Hold several seconds or longer.

Finish: Return to start position.

Sitting Spine-and-Leg Stretch

ELEPHANT WALK

Start: Stand.

1. Bend body at waist, keeping legs straight as hands are placed, palms down on the mat, in front of feet.

2. With arms and legs kept straight, begin a "walk," elephant style, lumbering from side to side.

Finish: Erect stand, arms at side.

Elephant Walk

SHOULDER STAND

Start: Lying position, arms at sides, palms down.
1. Slowly raise legs, keeping knees rigid, toes pointed.
2. Rotate legs toward head until they are parallel to the mat.
3. Slowly straighten body, extending legs upward and keeping arms flat on mat, palms down.
4. When body is in good balance, weight on shoulders, extend arms carefully outward to sides, keeping them on the mat, palms down.
5. Hold for several seconds.
6. Reverse action, making slow return to mat.

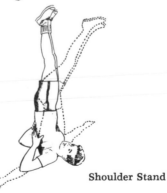

Shoulder Stand

Finish: Lying position.

Variation: In hold position, bend one leg and place sole of foot against knee of the straight leg; *or* in hold position, spread legs out to sides.

22

Spot on back and leg, from either side.

It is helpful, at first, to place hands on the hips to aid in establishing balance on the shoulders. All holds in a legs-up position increase circulation to the glands of the neck and head, and, therefore, are most beneficial.

TRIPOD BALANCE

Start: Squat.
1. Place hands flat on mat, palms down, forward and to sides of feet, fingers pointing forward.
2. Lower head slowly to mat and place forward portion of head on mat.
3. With head and arms sharing body weight equally, straighten the legs, raising torso until perpendicular to mat, hips flexed.
4. Spread legs slightly, keeping knees rigid, toes pointed.
5. Hold several seconds.
6. Make slow descent to mat.
Finish: Squat. Erect stand.

Spot on leg and small of back.

Slowness of execution should be stressed because it serves to develop excellent control, coordination, and balance.

Variation: Place the top of the head on the mat, flat-top fashion. This makes balancing more difficult.

Tripod Balance

TIP-UP BALANCE

Start: Squat.
1. As in the first step of the tripod balance, place hands on mat, palms down, forward and to sides of feet, fingers pointing forward.

23

2. Tip the body forward slightly, head up, the arms bearing the entire weight.
3. Bend the elbows slightly. At the same time, bend the knees and place them on the inner side of the arms, upper-elbow area.
4. Keeping head raised and toes pointed, achieve balance.

Finish: Return slowly to squat; then erect stand.

Spot on arm and shoulder.

Tip-up Balance

HEADSTAND

Start: Kneel on mat, hands flat on mat, fingers pointing forward.

1. Tip body forward until forward portion of the head touches mat.
2. As most of the weight shifts to head and hands, straighten legs, thus raising the torso.

Headstand

3. As body slowly assumes a tripod balance on head and hands, spread the legs slightly.
4. Keeping the legs rigid and the toes pointed, straighten the body, carefully maintaining balance until the body is fully extended.

5. Hold several seconds.
6. Return slowly to squat.
Finish: Erect stand.
Variation: While in hold, spread legs to split; *or* while in hold,
    cross legs yoga (lotus) style, or in other position student
    may prefer.

This method is preferred over the kickup for two reasons:
(1) In the event balance is lost, body is in tuck position most
of the time, thus preventing a landing flat on the back; (2)
it avoids overbalancing caused by too forceful a kick-off.

Spot carefully on back and leg.

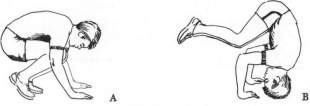

Forward Roll on Head

FORWARD ROLL ON HEAD (for the Young Child)

Start: Squat.
1. Place head on mat and assume tuck position.
2. Execute a push-off with both feet, arms trailing overhead.
3. Make a forward roll.
Finish: Sit. Erect stand.

This method is used only for the first few attempts. It
helps to educate the muscles of the neck, thus preventing
looseness of neck muscles and consequent injury.

FORWARD ROLL — TUCK-AND-DROP METHOD

Start: Squat.
1. Tuck head well in to chest. Place hands well in front of
    feet, fingers forward.
2. Lower body slowly, arms bending as they bear weight and
    prepare to transfer it to the neck and shoulders.
3. With knees bent tight to chest, *chin on chest*, begin roll.

25

Weight will be smoothly transferred from arms to neck and shoulders as body rolls forward.

Finish: Sit. Erect stand, without assistance from hands.

The term "tuck-and-drop" is somewhat a misnomer, as there is no actual drop involved, but rather a gradual transfer of weight. Once this method is thoroughly learned, the roll can be continued with sufficient force for the performer to grasp shins and finish in a squat.

Spot on back for both types of rolls. Use one hand under the neck the first few times. Always use mats.

Variation: Sequence of forward rolls; or backward roll:
From a sit on the mat, extend hands over shoulders, elbows bent and pointing forward. With head tucked to chest, body in full tuck, roll body backward. As rotation continues, let hands receive body weight by pushing downward, thereby lifting the body to let the head pass freely.

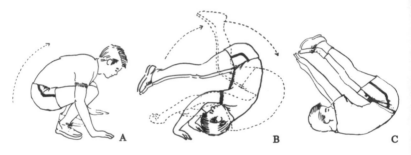

Forward Roll—Tuck-and-Drop Method

TORSO ROCK

Start: Lying position, face down, arms at side.
1. Bend knees; extend arms backward.
2. Grasp the insteps. As the legs attempt to straighten, they will pull the arms.
3. Begin to rock body backward and forward, holding head up.

Finish: Lying position.

Since this is difficult for some children, grasping of the insteps and arching the back will be sufficient success for the first few attempts.

26

Torso Rock

THE ROCKER

Start: Two children sit facing each other.
1. One partner spreads legs apart as the other moves close enough to place his legs between, then out and over the outspread legs.
2. With feet placed on either side of the partner's buttocks, both partners partially bend legs.
3. Both partners extend arms straight forward and grasp upper part of the partner's arm.
4. One member leans back as the other is raised from mat, his weight being transferred to his feet.
5. Partners reverse action and continue rocking.
Finish: Stop motion. Separate from partner.

Once the rocking is begun, the feet may be placed beneath the buttocks of the partner and remain there throughout the stunt.

The Rocker

Start: Stand, with hands holding firmly to some stationary object.

1. Raise one leg slowly as high as possible.
2. Bend body forward, head held high, knees rigid, toes pointed until body is parallel to mat, the legs in a 90-degree angle.
3. Hold.

Finish: Return to stand.

Variation: When this stunt has been well learned, two persons may face each other, grasp hands, and perform the scale, each lending some support to the other.

Double Forward Scale

FULL SPINAL ARCH

Start: Lying position, arms at sides.

Full Spinal Arch

1. Raise arms above head, bend elbows and place hands flat on mat behind shoulders, the fingers pointing toward the shoulders. Avoid placing the arms too close to the head.
2. Bend knees and place feet close to the buttocks.
3. Bear weight equally on arms and legs. Body will rise, spine fully arched, head bending backward, neck taut.
4. Hold for several seconds.

Finish: Return slowly to lying position.

SUPINE ARCH

Start: Sit.
1. Extend arms backward; place hands well behind buttocks, fingers pointing toward or away from buttocks.
2. Raise body slowly, head arched, legs straight with toes pointed.
3. Continue the rise until back is fully arched.
4. Hold.

Finish: Return slowly to sit.

Variation: Raise one leg; bend knee; place foot on other knee.

Supine Arch

SIDE-REST BALANCE

Start: Supine arch or sit with arms extended backward.
1. Turn body to one side, one arm and side of one foot supporting body weight.
2. Place free arm along side of body, or extend arm upward. Turn head to enable eyes to focus on hand.
3. Hold.

Finish: Roll sideways into forward-lean rest, body straight, and supported by straight arms and tops of feet.

Side-Rest Balance

BENT-KNEE SHOOT THROUGH

Start: Forward lean rest.

1. Bring legs forward, knees bent, toes pointed.
2. Assume tuck position as hips rise.
3. Let arms support weight of body. Hold head up.
4. Bend legs and pass them beneath body. Straighten legs as they are extended forward.

Finish: Sit.

Because a great deal of flexibility is required for this exercise, some children may find it quite difficult. Practicing a gradual walk-up with knees bent, weight shifting to arms as feet pass under body, is helpful in learning this stunt.

Bent-Knee Shoot Through

Start: Sit.
1. Body erect, head up and legs straight, raise legs slowly.
2. Extend arms, held straight, out to sides.
3. Knees rigid and toes pointed, lift legs as high as possible, keeping the knees together.
4. Balance body on buttocks.
5. Hold.
Finish: Return slowly to sit.

V-Seat

UNBRACED BACKWARD LEAN

Start: Sit.
1. Clasp hands behind the head.
2. Lean body backward as slowly as balance will allow, keeping legs rigid and flat on mat, with toes pointed.
3. Hold.
Finish: Return to sit. Make slow pull-up.
Variation: Hold arms up and out, in "V" fashion.

At first the legs may be held by spotters, but it is preferable that the lean be limited rather than dependent on outside support.

Unbraced Backward Lean

Start: Body bent, arms extended toward mat.

1. Approach from side and thrust arms to mat, one after the other.
2. Swing up outer leg as other leg pushes off. As weight shifts from one hand to the other, the body will rise from mat in flexed position.
3. Land on leading leg.

Finish: Return to stand.

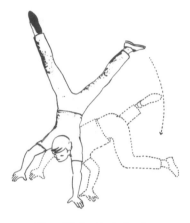

Flexed-Hip Cartwheel

FULL CARTWHEEL

Start: Stand with feet spread.

1. Approach from side, extend arms to sides and rock body weight onto right foot. (Start may be made with opposite leg.)
2. Lift left foot from mat, returning forcefully as right leg swings up.
3. Bend body down sharply as one hand after the other touches mat. Keep eyes on right hand, while extended legs pass directly overhead.
4. Push off with right arm as right foot returns to mat, followed by the left foot. Weight now returns to both legs.

Finish: Erect stand.

Spot with hands on waist, using cross-arm grip. This grip

can be simulated by grasping a child-width box between extended hands. The box is turned upside down, arms crossing without moving the hands. This is the grip used at the *beginning* of cartwheel. As the spotter follows the child through the stunt, the arms uncross and are parallel at the end of the stunt.

The use of the safety belt is a great help to the reluctant and a safety precaution for the overconfident.

HANDSTAND

Start: Semi-squat, one leg extended backward, hands on mat.
1. Kick up with extended leg, as bent leg pushes off from mat.
2. Holding head up, arch the back. Legs should be kept straight, and toes pointed. As balance is achieved, bring legs together.
3. Hold.

A

B

Handstand

C

33

Finish: Return to semi-squat; then to erect stand.

Spot with hand on the legs (and back, if necessary). Leading leg is grasped at ankle and both feet held when they meet.

It is helpful if student works up to the full-balance position in stages, by kicking up weakly at first and increasing force of takeoff, until the feel of the stunt comes to him. Practice should be with a safety belt, spotter, or, after some experience, against a wall. This is to prevent overbalancing and landing on the mat in a prone position—an accident which can knock the wind out of a child and enthusiasm for the handstand as well.

If the child advances to this point, he has acquired an excellent background for any sport and is undoubtedly in good physical condition. Some youngsters may never complete the full basic series. The natively less agile child is easily recognized by his movements. His achievements should be measured accordingly. Whether the student should advance to the intermediate level depends on his aptitude and interest.

Poses for Variety

From these basic skills, numerous interesting stunt combinations can be devised. The following examples will bring to mind many other stunt combinations:

a. Shoulder stand flanked by two horizontal spine stretches
b. Head stand flanked by two V-seats
c. Head stand flanked by two tip-up balances
d. V-seat flanked by two supine arches
e. Forward scale flanked by two unbraced back leans
f. Tripod balance flanked by two side-rest balances
g. Two handstands supported by central standing figure, whose raised arms grasp the feet. The pose forms an "M" shape, the handstands being the outer legs, the central figure the "Y" shape.
h. Three forward scales (or perhaps as many as six) join hands at a central point to form a star shape.
i. A headstand or other type balance, at the center of a circle composed of unbraced back lean, supine arch, side-rest balance, etc.

INTERMEDIATE TUMBLING
AND FREE EXERCISE

Certain movements in intermediate-level tumbling sets, such as the split and the one-leg stand may prove too difficult for some students to master. Some persons are so formed that, even with much practice, the joints cannot bend to these extreme positions. However, the effort of attempting to master them and the partial success achieved can be beneficial and rewarding. In a physical-development program, success can only be measured in terms of the benefits gained by the student.

FORWARD SCALE

Start: Standing position, good posture.
1. Bend torso forward. Sweep arms forward up, until they are parallel to mat.
2. Raise one leg until arms and legs are in a straight line.
3. Hold for several seconds, legs straight, toes pointed, head up.
Finish: Return slowly to start position.

Holding onto a wall or other stable object is helpful during the initial learning stages.

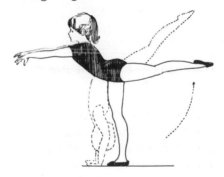

Forward Scale

Variation: Raise leg higher; hold longer, arms extended out to sides; *or* (for the very agile) needle scale: From forward scale, bend torso down until hands are flat on mat and forehead touches shin. Leg should extend straight up.

Start: Semi-squat, forearms flat on mat, palms down.
1. Extend one leg back. Raise head.
2. Kick-up with extended leg, pushing off with other leg. Kick-off brings body up into full stand position, back well arched.
3. Hold several seconds; legs straight, toes pointed.
Finish: Return to semi-squat, followed by stand.
   Spot as for handstand.

Forearm Stand

FORWARD DROP

Start: Stand, arms extended forward and up.
1. Extend one leg backward and upward.
2. Make a slow lean forward, arms leading.
3. As body drops forward to mat, touch hands down flat.
4. Bend elbows deeply to absorb shock.
5. Sweep up raised leg as high as possible.
6. Hold; head raised, leg extended straight, toes pointed.
Finish: Push arms against mat and straighten, raising body into front-lean support.

   It is wise to have a padding of two mats for extra safety. This is a dramatic lead into a number of movements. It is also very effective when used in poses, such as those outlined below.

Forward Drop

Three-Person Poses

a. Forward scale flanked by two forearm stands
b. Forward scale flanked by two forward drops with hold
c. Forearm stand flanked by forward scales

ONE-ARM SIDE SUPPORT

Start: Forward-lean position.
1. Turn body to right as right arm is extended upward.
2. Hold this arm straight, thumb turned in and against palm.
3. Free leg rests on supporting left leg, which bears the weight on the outer side of the foot.
4. Raise head and look at the tip of extended arm.
5. Hold.
Finish: Return to forward lean or sit, arms out to sides, legs straight.
Variation: Raise free leg as high as possible while in hold position.

37

One-Arm Side Support

SEMI-SPLIT WITH FORWARD LEAN (Modified Straddle Lean)

Start: Sit, legs extended straight forward.
1. Spread legs to the sides as far as possible.
2. Keep knees straight, toes pointed.
3. Lean body forward as arms spread to sides. Grasp ankles, or a spot higher on shin if any strain is involved.
4. Hold head up.
Finish: Start position.
Variation (for the very agile): Spread in a full front split.

Semi-Split with Forward Lean

SPLIT

Start: Standing position.
1. Spread legs apart; one sliding forward, the other backward.
2. If possible, keep knees straight.
3. Extend arms to sides at 45 or 90 degree angle.
4. Slowly lower body as legs spread wide.

5. When extreme spread, or widest position possible without strain, is reached, touch hands to floor if support is needed.
6. Hold, head high, back erect.

Finish: Bend knees as lower leg slides to one side. Rise on either knee, hands helping, or assume sit position.

Though many students will not be able to achieve the full position, they should be encouraged to go as far as they can, then lean the torso and head back in an impressive pose. Girls may use any number of graceful arm positions while boys may extend arms out to sides, palms down. Rear knee may be bent if desired. Finish with rear knee bending to bear body weight. Rise to stand, or lower to mat for sit.

Split

SHOOT THROUGH

Start: Forward-lean rest.
1. Bend hips as both legs are brought forward, arms bearing body weight, head up.
2. Keep legs as straight as possible; swing them between arms.

Shoot Through

Finish: Sit position, arms behind buttocks, head leaned back.

Spot from side. Place hands on either side of the waist and lift up as the hips are bent and raised. This action is difficult for many children, and they will need assistance at first.

ONE-LEG STAND

Start: Stand.
1. Raise one leg off to side and bend knee.
2. With arm on same side, grasp sole of foot at arch from the front.
3. Straighten leg; point toes; raise leg.
4. Extend other arm up, palm facing in.
Finish: Stand.

It is good to practice with one arm on a wall for balance, until some skill is developed.

One-Leg Stand

More Three-Person Poses

a. Split flanked by two one-leg stands.
b. Headstand flanked by two one-arm side supports.
c. Headstand with legs in split flanked by two splits.
d. Handstand flanked by two knee scales.

It is apparent that a great number of such combinations using three or more persons can be devised. Students should be encouraged to develop a good repertoire.

Start: Stand position.
1. Bend body forward. Place hands flat on mat, as for hand-stand.
2. Bend one knee; extend other leg backward.
3. Swing extended leg backward and up, as other leg pushes off with good thrust and follows suit.
4. Arch back to the extreme as the leading leg nears mat. (Legs never come together during the walkover.)

Walkover

5. Thrust hips up and over, as hands push off from mat.
6. Leading leg touches mat first, followed by trailing leg which stops in front of it.

Finish: Stand.

For best results, use the towel or rope safety belt. This gives confidence and can mean the difference between success and failure. Full effort is more easily given when danger of falling is eliminated.

Variation: Begin with handstand. Execute a split in the handstand, followed by the completion of the walkover. This is aided by a strong whip of the legs.

The walkover is used primarily as a stunt for girls; boys

often do not have the necessary flexibility required for the walkover and its cousin the backbend. The backbend is expanded into the back walkover—a reversal of the front walkover.

Start: Short run-in and skip.
1. Immediately thrust straight arms downward to mat, using entire force of arms and shoulders.
2. Make a strong kick-off, one leg behind the other. Snap hips up and over as they straighten. (A rapid straightening of body combined with an up-and-over thrust of hips snaps the body over. A slight bend of the knees is helpful to some children.)

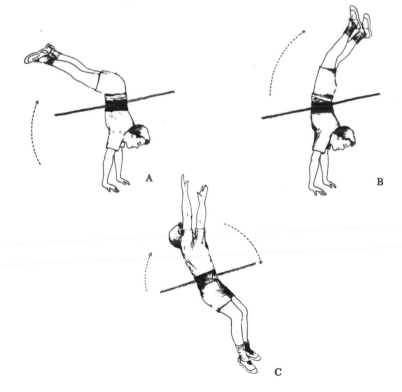

Handspring

3. Bring legs together, as straight as possible, back arching, arms stretched straight. Hold head backward throughout.
4. With body straight, force of arms and shoulders plus momentum of legs will carry body through to a stand.

Finish: Erect stand, arms extended forward, or to the sides for balance.

Variation: A more advanced stunt is the double-leg takeoff with a mule-kick motion. It is executed as above, except that, instead of a skip, both legs hit the mat and bound off simultaneously.

Spot, using the towel or rope safety belt, or a standard safety belt.

When these stunts have been mastered, the basic building blocks of tumbling have been acquired. With growing skill and confidence, artistic routines may be compiled, even by the young child, especially when encouraged to follow the course of individual preference. Lack of flexibility will go unnoticed in a routine based on grace and imagination.

4

❀ ❀ ❀

MARCHING MANEUVERS

Training in marching maneuvers is most helpful when dealing with large groups. Knowledge of how to line up and form marching formations can be a lifesaver, in the event of a fire or some other emergency which demands rapid and orderly exit. Children who are trained in marching are less apt to panic at the thought of mass egress from a building.

Marching maneuvers can be made entertaining if the element of challenge becomes part of the training. Once the basics are mastered, just standing the children in a line before the instructor and challenging the class to a duel of the senses proves highly entertaining to the students. A series of rapid-fire commands: "Left Turn!" "About Face!" "To the Rear March!" "Right Turn!" is fun for all, as the class tries to prove itself more accomplished than its challenger.

As skill improves, the older children can be taught to form various geometric patterns. Marching maneuvers also are the basis of calisthenics. They serve to position the group, so as to prevent the students from injuring each other by being in too close proximity to one another.

1. Bring legs together, feet pointing forward.
2. Straighten arms, palms facing body.
3. Hold back and head erect, and abdomen flat.

This is the basic command of marching, usually used when the group is lined up, side by side, facing instructor.

AT EASE

Start: Attention or other stance.
1. Move left leg about one foot to the left side, distributing weight equally.
2. Place arms behind the back, palms crossed, one hand gripping the other. Retain good posture.

RIGHT DRESS

Start: Attention position.
1. Raise left arm and place palm on the left hip. (Group should shift outward, as necessary, to allow ample space for this position without actual body contact.)
2. Turn head to the right and straighten line.

A turning of the head without the arm action is called "Eyes Right" or "Eyes Left." This is used in order to straighten a line already properly spaced.

Attention   At Ease   Right Dress

LEFT DRESS

This is the opposite of right dress.

FORWARD MARCH

Start: Attention position.
1. Smart walk, always starting with left foot.
2. Marchers proceed in direction they are facing at time of command.

HALT

Start: Forward or rear march, skip, etc.
1. After command "Halt!" is given, take one more step.
2. Close feet in stop.
   Because of the last two movements, each taking one beat, the command is often: "Halt! One, Two."

Open Ranks

OPEN RANKS

Start: Attention, in a line, or in some other formation.
1. Upon command, step sideways to either side of formation center.
2. When rank is fairly well spread apart each child extends both arms out to the sides.
3. When fingertips barely touch, the command has been correctly executed.

46

This is generally followed by, "Attention!" The open ranks maneuver is used when calisthenics are to be performed, and follows the execution of three-, four-, or five-abreast formations. Opening of ranks eliminates the chance of inadvertent body contact during the ensuing activity.

CLOSE RANKS

This is the opposite of open ranks.
Start: Open ranks position.
1. Upon command, retrace original steps of open ranks, arms at sides.
2. When back to original or desired position, the command has been fully executed.
3. "Halt!"

Return need not be to original position. The group may be facing another direction or may be stopped before ranks have been completely closed. Forming ranks is shown on page 48. Open, closed, and partially open ranks are on page 49.

MARK TIME

Start: Forward or rear march.

To the beat of the march, take steps without moving forward or backward. As in the case of "Halt!" two steps precede execution of command. With the command, "Mark time, *mark*," the command is executed on the last word, "mark."
1. On command, "Mark Time," take two steps in unison with command.
2. On final word of command, "Mark," take next step in place, and continue marching in place until another command is given.

RIGHT FACE

Start: Attention in any formation.
1. Upon command, pivot both feet to the right. (Pivot points are the ball of left foot and the heel of right foot.)
2. When the quarter turn is completed, lift left foot slightly off floor and place it next to the right (weight-bearing) foot.
3. Assume attention again. The command is now fully executed.

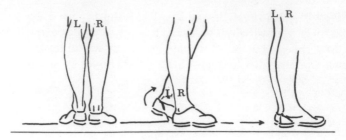

Right Face

LEFT FACE

This is executed in exactly the same manner as right face, except in the opposite direction, the left foot being the weight-bearing foot.

FORMING RANKS (to the left)

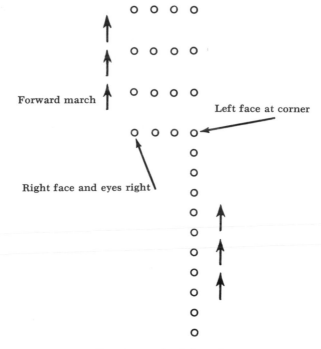

Forming ranks of four abreast

Forming Ranks

48

Closed ranks

Partially opened ranks

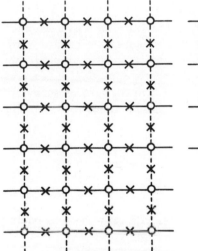

Opening ranks both ways

Opening ranks sideways

"x" indicates where outstretched arms of pupils just barely touch (See figure on page 46 for open ranks stance)

"o" represents one child

Line to either side of "o" represents outstretched arms

Open, Closed, and Partially Open Ranks

Start: Forward march, one child behind the other.
1. On the command, "Form Ranks to the Left," take two or three more steps, ending with weight on right foot.

2. Pivot body to the left on ball of right foot. This will be the pivot point for forming all other ranks.
3. Step forward on left foot, followed with one good-sized step for each child in rank.

NOTE: At this point, the desired number of children in rank is indicated by voice. (A hand signal may be given along with original command.)

4. After required number of steps, execute right face. Marcher is now facing in direction of original march.
5. Marking time, leader turns head to the right and waits for designated number of persons to follow suit and line up next to him.
6. Rank completed, march forward.

The time spent by each rank in waiting for all its members to take their positions spaces the lines nicely. Forming ranks to the right is done in reverse fashion. A little practice soon makes this a smooth, rapid, and orderly operation. It is a good idea for the instructor to place an arm forward of each rank until the rank is complete, then motion them forward. This lessens confusion during learning.

ABOUT FACE

Start: Attention position.
1. Place right foot behind left foot, with only the toes resting on floor.
2. With weight on balls of feet, execute a full half turn.

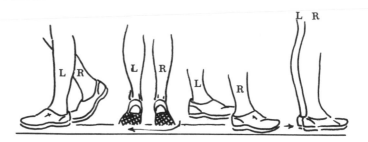

About Face

3. Shift body weight onto the full soles.
4. Move left foot forward, ending behind the right foot, and close in. Weight is then borne on right foot.

Variation: Cross-Leg About Face

    a. Cross right foot in front of left foot, ending with toes even and next to each other.

    b. Rise onto balls of both feet and execute a full half turn.

Finish: Feet even and next to each other.

This can be reversed and executed in the opposite direction, left foot crossing over the right, and followed by the half-turn pivot.

TO THE REAR MARCH

Start: Marching forward.

1. At the word "March," in the command, "To the Rear March," the leg stepping forward assumes body weight.

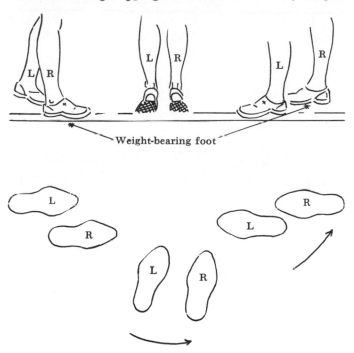

Weight-bearing foot

To the Rear March

2. Rise onto balls of both feet and execute a full half turn. Leg bearing body weight is still the same, but it is now the rear leg.
3. Forward leg now takes a step forward, as weight is shifted onto it.

The maneuver is done on two counts. Count "One" is the rise to balls of feet and pivot; count "Two" is the forward step which resumes the march in the opposite direction. Some children prefer to lift the free foot clear of the floor at end of pivot before taking the forward step.

Using these basics, many geometric patterns and designs can be formed. A well-trained drill team is an asset to any school. It is a rewarding personal experience to be a member of such a team.

5

❋ ❋ ❋

APPARATUS
WORK:
EQUIPMENT
AND ITS
ADJUSTMENT

APPARATUS ACTIVITIES

Both elementary and high school students enjoy apparatus activities. "This is fun," is the first reaction, and indeed it is.

The instruction of children in apparatus work differs considerably from the techniques appropriate for adults, a factor which has prompted the preparation of this manual. Since apparatus must be adjusted to the child's requirements, a section on "Equipment and Its Adjustment" appears in this chapter.

Differences between apparatus activities appropriate for girls and those appropriate for boys are clearly detailed in the stunts or exercises outlined on the following pages. Exercises for girls are formulated to develop a strong, supple body, with emphasis on balance, poise, timing, endurance, and flexibility, rather than strength. Girls of six or seven can do surprisingly well after several months of activity on the apparatus. Teen-age girls find apparatus work exciting and challenging to both mind and body.

Throughout the elementary and intermediate stages, boys should be encouraged to use the arms as much as possible, especially at ages eight through twelve. The stunt routine for older boys can be supplemented with uprises, which will develop excellent muscular tone in the upper torso. Push-ups should be a part of the elementary training for boys. Once mastered on the floor, push-ups may be performed on parallel bars. After puberty, a crotch support should be worn by boys. Of course, no child with a hernia should be allowed to participate in these sports until the hernia has been corrected.

Older boys will advance through the elementary stages of apparatus activities more quickly than younger boys. Their interest usually becomes intense, which is, after all, the chief determining factor. Even children with handicaps can do well in some of the events. For instance, one of the Amateur Athletic Union's top performers on the rings was a war veteran who had lost a leg.

Good health, however, is a prime requisite of all sports activities. It is not advisable to pressure children beyond their capabilities. Overweight children who have difficulty with apparatus work can usually master the basics. For the less agile, group games, marching maneuvers, rope jumping, or volleyball will help to round out physical development (see the chapter on games).

The line between elementary and intermediate apparatus activity is difficult to define. Although the exercises are presented in what is believed to be the order of difficulty, individual differences in muscle development may make one stunt easier for certain students than a stunt which appears simpler to perform.

In any case, by the time students reach what is here indicated as the intermediate level of apparatus work, attention should be given to certain details of style. The approach to the apparatus and the terminating walk should take on a polished look. All corners required in the approach to the apparatus should be squared, and posture should be excellent. Before the apparatus is mounted, the performer should pause momentarily in the attention postion, at which time he composes himself.

When leaving the apparatus, the student should walk to the end of the mat, make a well-squared turn, return to his place in the line, and assume an at-ease position. Students should remain in line, well back from the apparatus, at ease, in good order. This procedure is not only pleasing to the eye but is a matter of safety and discipline in the gym or recreation area.

EQUIPMENT AND ITS ADJUSTMENT

Since most athletic equipment is designed for use by adults, adjustment and modification are necessary to make it suitable for children. It is, therefore, important for the instructor to be informed about the apparatus and its potentials.

It should be noted that standard playground equipment has many possibilities in providing apparatus for children. Swing equipment makes an excellent support for the portable indoor-outdoor rings. Lawn areas can be used for tumbling, sand pits for the high jump and the broad jump. A number of pieces of equipment can be constructed of lumber: namely, the high-jump equipment, the beatboard, the balance beam, and the hurdles. A mat wrapped around the balance beam makes it suitable for vaulting. Parallel bars (for limited use) and the horizontal bar can be made of galvanized steel pipe and fittings, with the bases embedded in concrete.

Methods of adjusting standard equipment or of making simple apparatus are considered below.

Balance Beam

A regulation balance beam, which stands four feet from the floor, can be lowered by constructing shorter sawhorses. Make sure that screws rather than nails are used in assembling the parts. To prevent slipping, nail or glue pieces of rubber to the underside of the sawhorse legs.

A low beam for the very young, and for general practice, should measure about one foot from the floor to the top of the beam. A good height for the balance beam to be used for girls of intermediate-grade level is 34 inches from the floor. For this height, make the legs of the sawhorses 31 inches long.

Side Horse Adjustment

The standard side horse is too high, even at its lowest point of adjustment, for children in the lower elementary grades to mount. A large springboard can give youngsters help up to the level needed for performance on this apparatus. Another way to overcome the height problem is to construct a set of sturdy, low sawhorses and use the balance beam, wrapped with a small mat which has been secured at each end with ropes or straps. An ordinary beam, 4 inches by 6 inches, may be substituted for the balance beam.

A side horse, which has pommels, is easier for children to work with, as it gives them something to grasp. Most side horses have removable pommels.

Side Horse with Springboard

Rings

Wooden rings are ideal for children. They are lightweight and easy to work with. They should be wound with *nonplastic* adhesive tape for safe, sure grip. The tape can be removed and replaced when it becomes worn or soiled. Under no circumstances should the thin metal rings, so commonly found in playgrounds, be used in the activities outlined in this manual. Such rings are painful to use.

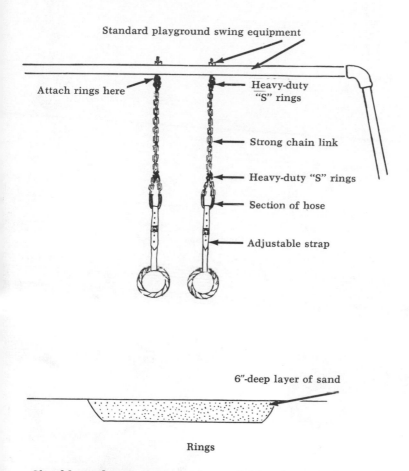

Standard playground swing equipment

Attach rings here

Heavy-duty "S" rings

Strong chain link

Heavy-duty "S" rings

Section of hose

Adjustable strap

6"-deep layer of sand

Rings

Should regulation rings not be available, rings can be made which are portable and suitable for outdoor use. Since they

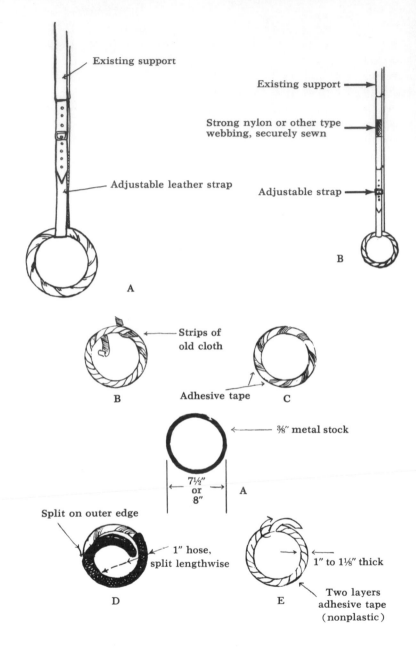

Existing support

Existing support →

Strong nylon or other type
webbing, securely sewn →

Adjustable leather strap

Adjustable strap →

B

A

Strips of
old cloth

Adhesive tape

B

C

⅜″ metal stock

7½″
or
8″

A

Split on outer edge

1″ hose,
split lengthwise

1″ to 1⅛″ thick

Two layers
adhesive tape
(nonplastic)

D

E

Making Rings

can be attached to and removed from playground equipment (see figure A, p. 58), they are practical for the school that has no gym.

Rings are usually sold with manila rope, but heavy ¾-inch cotton or nylon rope is more satisfactory. Chain link is also used and has the advantage of being durable enough for use outdoors. If rings cannot be lowered sufficiently for use with small children, they can be simply and inexpensively adjusted as illustrated on page 58.

For outdoor rings, the dirt under the rings should be dug out to a depth of 6 inches and replaced with a 6-inch layer of sand. If the rings are used for swinging, as in "Intermediate Work on the Rings," a long strip under the rings should be padded in this manner.

Rope Adjustment

A standard rope can be used by children of all ages, since it reaches to the ground. If an indoor rope is not available, the playground swing supports can be used to support a 1-inch manila rope, attached lasso style. The ground below the rope should be dug out to a depth of 6 inches and replaced with sand. This makes an excellent pad, an important safety factor.

Parallel Bars with Stacked Mats

Parallel Bars

A quality set of parallel bars will adjust to a height suitable for children. If bars do not lower sufficiently, stack mats under the bars.

When contemplating the purchase of parallel bars, take a searching look into what is available. Junior tubular-steel parallel bars have recently appeared on the market.

In parallel bars, the test of quality is in the adjustment mechanism. Stability, ease of adjustment, and range of adjustment should be carefully checked. The bars should adjust to the width of the shoulders of a young child. One bar should extend to a height of 7½ feet. An auxiliary bar can be obtained to accommodate this height, but it is an added expense. Also check whether the adjustment mechanism has a solid lock and whether the apparatus can be easily moved to and from the area of activity.

Indoor Horizontal Bar

The regulation horizontal bar can be adjusted in height from 8 feet to 3 feet. There should be little if any height problem. If there is, stack mats under the bar.

High Jump

Regulation high-jump standards do not adjust to a level low enough for young children. A triangular-shaped metal rod is

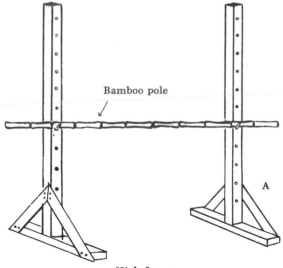

Bamboo pole

A

High Jump

often used as a bar. The substitution of a bamboo rod is highly recommended, since it is lightweight and bounces away from the jumper easily.

Modifying the standards and replacing or duplicating them is illustrated in figures B, C and D, below). Drilling of additional holes at a downward angle, as shown, with allow the rod to be lowered to the required level. In this way, any set of standards can be rendered suitable for the use of children.

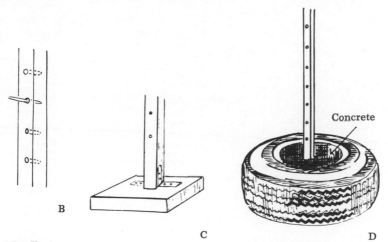

B

C

D

Concrete

Hurdles

Modifying or duplicating the hurdles is a simple matter. Drilling a number of holes near the bottom of the upright supports and in the horizontal board renders hurdles adjustable to the lowest heights needed. A wing-nut bolt to

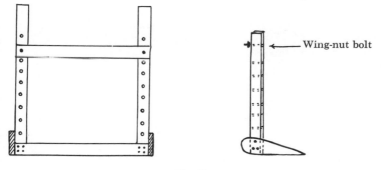

Wing-nut bolt

Hurdles

fasten the board at the desired height makes rapid readjustment possible.

The illustration on p. 61 shows the construction of hurdles. Wooden pegs or nails may be inserted into drilled holes to support a bamboo pole. When constructing the bases, care must be taken to assure that the hurdles topple easily. This is dependent upon the degree of curvature in the base supports.

6

❀ ❀ ❀

RINGS

Exercises on the rings develop timing, coordination, and agility. They also strengthen the muscles of the arms and abdomen. Children can begin work on the rings as early as first grade, provided that the rings can be lowered to the height of their shoulders.

On the elementary level, both boys and girls follow much the same pattern of exercises, except that boys should be encouraged to condition themselves to doing at least ten chin-ups. Girls will not need to do that many. There need be no concern that girls will develop oversized arm muscles. Their work on the rings is based on circles or swings from a hang position or on movements from a sit or a free hang. The exercises are specifically calculated to develop strength in the abdominal area.

The chapter which covers equipment and its adjustment includes a discussion of indoor and outdoor rings and their possible modification. Points on safety and spotting are also treated in the respective chapters on those topics. Review these subjects carefully before beginning the work on the rings.

It is important to remember that, before strength is developed in the arms, the performer may suddenly release his grip. The spotter should stand to one side and slightly back of the performer, with hands in position to make a fast catch. A padding of two mats should be placed under the indoor rings. The dirt under outdoor rings should be dug out and replaced with sand. (See "Rings" in chapter on equipment.)

The apparatus should not be used without supervision. Indoor rings should be hoisted to the ceiling when not in use. Outdoor rings should be removed from the supports and stored indoors. A safety check of the chain link should be made regularly.

ELEMENTARY WORK ON THE RINGS

Basic Movements

THE GRIP

Start: Stand directly below rings, arms extended upward.
1. Place hands on rings from outside, palms facing toward the performer. Curl thumbs around rings from beneath.
2. Lock fingers down around rings.

Unless specified otherwise, this grip is used in all exercises on this apparatus. To assist in maintaining a firm grip, chalk is rubbed on the hands *before* using the rings.

Ring Grip

Basic Exercises

CHIN POSITION

Start: Stand below rings, adjusted within easy arm's reach.
1. Raise arms and grip rings firmly.

64

2. Make slow pull-up into chin position, elbows fully bent.
3. Keep legs straight; point toes.

Finish: Return slowly to start position.

Some children may not be able to do more than one chin-up on the first attempt.

Spot with both hands at waist of child.

Chin Position

Form should be demonstrated and mentioned from the beginning of the work on the rings. Until each movement is fully mastered, however, it is not desirable to stress form unduly.

HIP CIRCLE IN CHIN POSITION

Start: Chin position, executed slowly, rings just above head.

Hip Circle in Chin Position

1. With upper torso stationary, rotate the hips.
2. Hold legs together, toes pointed and knees straight.
3. After three to five complete circles, stop motion.

Finish: Descend slowly to mat.

Variation: Rotate hips in opposite direction. After the hip circle is mastered in each direction, two motions may be combined into one exercise.

SWING IN CHIN POSITION

Start: Slow pull-up into chin position, rings just above head.
1. Make a shallow swing of body, forward and back, from the waist.
2. Keep legs straight, toes pointed.
3. Make several swings, followed by a rest, still in chin position.
4. Make slow descent to mat.

At this point, the jump dismount can be introduced while the performer is still working on rings within arm's reach from the floor.

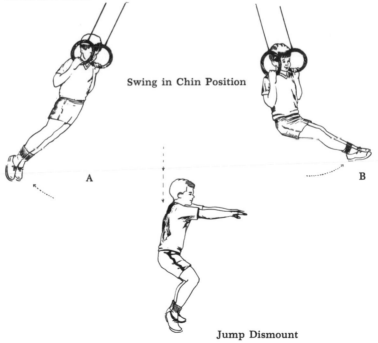

Swing in Chin Position

A

B

Jump Dismount

Start: Chin position or hang, toes off the ground.
1. Stop all motion. Keep legs straight and toes pointed.
2. Release grip and touch feet to the mat, toes first.
3. Bear weight on balls of the feet, and bend knees to cushion the landing.
Finish: Extend arms forward, parallel to the floor. Arms out to the sides is also acceptable.

Learning, in the beginning, to land properly pays dividends. To land on the heel or full foot invites ankle injuries.

BODY CIRCLE

Start: Stand below rings and grasp them firmly, rings adjusted above shoulders, but within easy reach.
1. Lean body forward or off to one side, toes on mat, legs straight.
2. Without moving the toes, inscribe a full circle with the body.
3. Make four to eight complete circles, ending with backward lean.

Body Circle

Finish: Pull into start position.
Variation: Exercises may be limited to a side-to-side motion.

Start: Grasp rings, set at shoulder height.
1. Kick up one leg, followed with the other.
2. Tense and flex arms somewhat, as if starting chin position.
3. Bend head back as body rotates backward.
4. When a steady balance in the flex position is achieved, legs straight, toes pointed, stop rotation.
NOTE: The knees may be bent during the backward rotation in the initial stages of learning but the stunt cannot be considered mastered until the legs can be held reasonably straight throughout the exercise. This is an important basic movement and should be learned well.
5. Hold full position. With practice, hold can be increased to several seconds.
6. Make slow return to mat, using abdominal muscles.
Finish: Start position.

Spot on arm and small of back for the ascent. It is helpful if the performer catches one foot on the ring, as the leading leg passes over the torso, thus preventing bounding back to the mat before rotation is complete. An assist from the spotter can assure at least partial success, which is highly desirable. In descent, the legs may come down heavily at first, but if the arms are tensed, chin-position fashion, strength will be gained

Upstart Position

in the abdominal area, and a slow, gentle return of the legs to the mat will be attained. Spotting on arm and leg is recommended.

ARM EXTENSION IN CHIN POSITION

Start: Pull-up into chin position, rings just above head.
1. Extend one arm to the side, keeping legs straight, toes pointed.
2. Return to chin position.
3. Drop to mat.
Finish: Erect stand below rings, arms at sides.
Variation: Extend one arm, then the other, and repeat.

Boys should eventually work up to four or five extensions with each arm, as one exercise. One or two arm extensions is enough for girls.

Arm Extension in Chin Position

KNEE HANG

Start: Upstart position, rings at shoulder level.
1. Place both legs in rings, knee-deep.
2. Bend knees. Spotter places hand on performer's insteps.
3. Release grip on rings.
4. Lower body slowly into full hang. Hold several seconds.

5. Make slow pull-up, using a slight whip of the arms for assistance.
6. Grasp rings with both hands.
7. Slip legs out of rings as upstart is resumed.

Finish: Drop to mat, erect stand.

It is often helpful if only one hand is lowered on the first few attempts, until confidence is gained.

Variation: When exercise is well learned, attempt to arch the back and touch the toes. By now, pull-up to regrasp the rings should depend wholly upon the abdominal muscles. The more agile may grasp the toes, with a momentary hold.

Spot on arm and back. Spot arm and instep when in hang.

Knee Hang

BIRD'S NEST

Start: Upstart position, rings at chest level.
1. Rotate body backward, as feet only are placed in rings.
2. Hook feet in rings at point of instep.
3. Continue rotation until back is in full arch, head up.
4. Hold for several seconds.
5. Bend head to chest as the hips are bent and rotation is reversed, ending in upstart position.

Finish: Make a slow descent to mat, using abdominal muscles only.

This motion may seem confusing at first, but after one or two attempts the child acquires the feel of it.

Spot on upper arm and waist.

Bird's Nest

BACKWARD HANG

Start: Upstart position, rings at shoulder level.
1. Continue backward rotation, legs straight, toes pointed, moving slowly until body can no longer continue.
2. Extend legs forward and up. Hold head up.

Backward Hang

3. Hold for several seconds, toes well pointed.

Finish: Drop to mat. Stand at attention.

Variation: From full back hang, a backward whip of legs and fast tuck of head to chest plus flexing of hips will return body to upstart.

Spot on upper arm and waist.

INVERTED HANG

Start: Upstart position, rings at shoulder level.
1. Straighten body slowly, legs straight, toes pointed.
2. Continue motion until, with body perpendicular to floor, and back arched, good balance is achieved.
3. Hold for several seconds.
4. Make slow return to upstart.

Finish: Make slow return to mat.

Variation: While in full inverted hang, bend one leg and place the sole of that foot on the knee of the straight leg.

Spot on upper arm and small of back.

Inverted Hang

BACKWARD SOMERSAULT

Start: Stand under rings, adjusted to chest level.
1. Kick off from mat into upstart position.

2. Continue slow backward motion, until feet touch the mat.
3. Retain grasp on rings and attempt to return to stand.
   a. Rotate shoulders in order to maintain grasp.
   b. Push arms out to the sides, so the body can return to the stand. This is the rotation involved in the dislocate covered later.

Finish: Stand, arms at sides.

Variation: Instead of rising to stand, flex the knees and, with a slight jump, reverse the rotation. Finish is in start position.

Spot on upper arm and small of back.

Backward Somersault

ONE-KNEE HANG WITH LEG EXTENSION

Start: Upstart position, rings at chest height.
1. Place right leg up to knee in right ring. Bend right knee.
2. Extend left leg forward, toes pointed.
3. Lean head back.
4. Arch back nicely.
5. Hold for several seconds.
6. Make slow return to upstart.

Finish: Descend slowly to mat.

Spot on upper arm and small of back.

Variation: Release right hand from ring and extend above
head.

One-Knee Hang with Leg Extension

FULL KNEE HANG TO SIT POSITION

leading into

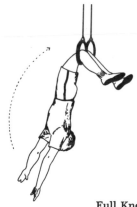

Full Knee Hang to Sit Position

This is an example of what can be done by combining four basic movements and adding variations.

Start: Upstart position, rings at chest level.

1. From upstart, place legs in rings up to knees.
2. Bend knees and release hands. Lower body into full knee hang.
3. With a smart whip of arms and a smooth pull of abdominal muscles, grasp webbing above rings as body swings up. (Grasping one ring, then the webbing on the other ring, facilitates learning.)
4. Pull body up into sit, legs straight, toes pointed. Hold.

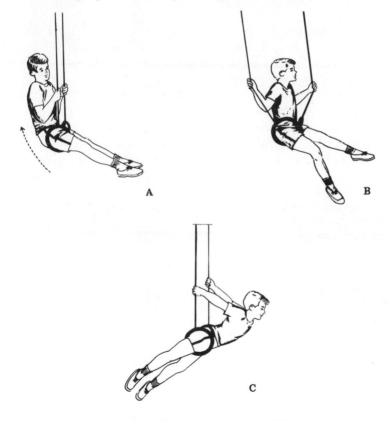

A   B

C

In-Ring Semi-Split to In-Ring Forward Lean

5. Spread legs. Push arms out to sides. Tense legs.
6. Body rises as weight is transferred to upper inner thighs.
7. Hold momentarily.
8. Make a slow forward lean, head up, back arched, legs straight, toes pointed. Hold.
9. Bring arms and legs forward as body leans back.
Finish: Make slow return to mat. Erect stand.
   Spot on upper arm and torso, as movement permits.

This covers the basic movements on the rings. They can be arranged in innumerable combinations and each child should be encouraged to compile routines all his own.

Stunts for Elementary Level

Once mastered, the stunts can be executed with rings raised, thus necessitating a strong jump in order to grasp them. This enables the child to swing into the upstart, and brings in the element of timing. Except for the body circle, all other stunts are identically performed, the swing-up replacing the kick-up.

The backward somersault should be done slowly at first and carefully spotted. As skill and timing improve, this will become a neat somersault dismount, which looks impressive.

Semi-Half Lever and Half Lever in Chin Position

SEMI-HALF LEVER AND HALF LEVER IN CHIN POSITION

Start: Pull up into chin position, rings at arms' reach.
1. Slowly raise legs as high as possible.
2. Hold; legs straight, toes pointed.
3. Make slow return to hang in chin position.
Finish: Neat drop to mat. Erect stand.

As muscle strength grows, the half lever can be achieved. It is not necessary to raise the legs to the full position to reap benefit from this movement.

STILL-RING SWING WITH FRONT AND BACK DISMOUNTS

Start: Jump up to rings, adjusted several inches above arms' reach.
1. Whip legs forward, then back.
2. Swing, legs straight, toes pointed.
3. Backward Dismount
   a. At height of backward swing, flex hips and release grip on rings.

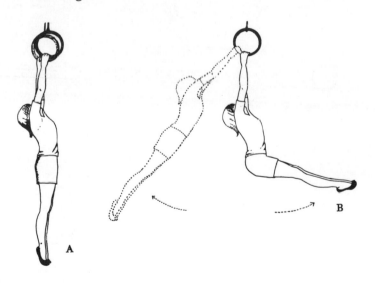

Still-Ring Swing

b. Drop to mat, toes leading, landing on balls of feet and bending knees to absorb shock.

4. Forward Dismount
    a. At height of forward swing, body arched, toes pointing to mat, release grip.
    b. Drop to mat, as above.

Spot with extended arm guard (see figure C, p. 10).
The forward-swing dismount must be well learned before

Still-Ring Swing Back Dismount

Still-Ring Swing Forward Dismount

it is used with rings in motion. When any swing is executed, mats must be placed so the entire movement, including dismount, is done above a padded area.

FORWARD SWING

Start: Stand below rings, within arms' reach. Swing is started with two steps back. This is indicated as the start position in the illustration which appears below.

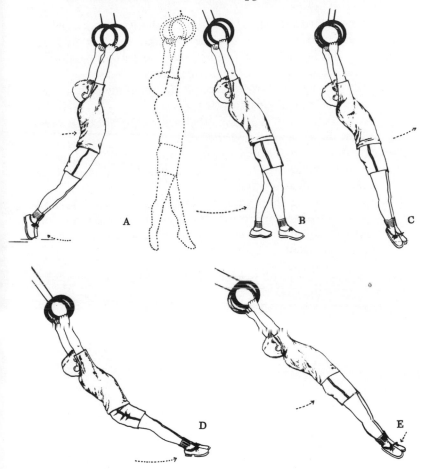

Forward Swing

1. Take two rapid steps forward, pushing off from the mat on the second step.
2. Arch body as legs extend backward.
3. Thrust legs forcefully forward, flexing the hips and leading with legs straight, toes pointed.
4. At height of forward swing, arch body in full layout, in preparation for the beginning of backward swing.

BACKWARD SWING

5. As backward motion begins, extend the legs backward.
6. As legs near mat, arch back and extend toes toward mat.
7. After the leading foot touches the mat, rapidly followed by the other, take two quick steps to the rear.
8. Push off vigorously with second leg, pushing body to the rear as both legs kick forward.
9. As the body swings higher, the legs swing backward, resulting in an arching of the back.
10. At height of backward swing, bend the body at hips as legs extend forward in preparation for the forward swing and the double-step push-off.

Finish: End swing by dragging soles of feet on the mat, on the backward swing only. Dragging the feet on the forward swing may cause injury, as there is less control in this movement.

A   B

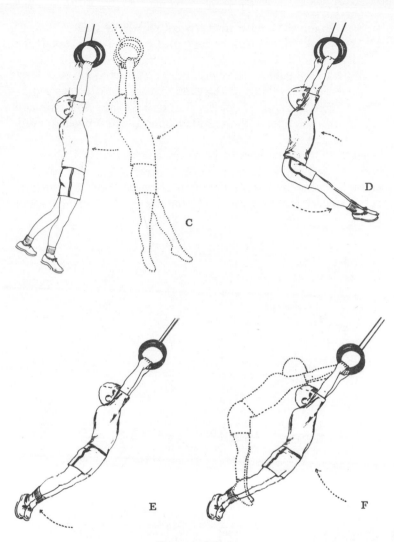

C

D

E

F

Backward Swing

FORWARD-SWING DISMOUNT FROM FLYING RINGS

Start: Position 3 of forward swing as body nears height of
forward swing.

1. Straighten body with no forward thrust of legs.
2. Arch back. With straight legs and pointed toes, reach for mat.
3. With knees bent to cushion shock, let toes touch mat first. Bear weight on balls of the feet, arms extended forward.

Finish: Erect stand, shoulders back, head up, and stomach tucked in. Spot with extended arm guard, if needed. (Figure C, p. 10)

At first, practice should be from a low swing. Unless the body is arched, with feet leading downward, the head or shoulders may hit the mat first. A mental image of trying to clear an obstacle and reaching for the ground on the other

Forward Swing Dismount from Flying Rings

side is helpful in learning a correct dismount. A decided down-ward point of the toes should be stressed. Timing is im-portant here.

INTERMEDIATE WORK ON THE RINGS

SINGLE KNEE CIRCLE WITH REGRIP

Start: Upstart position, rings at arms' reach.
1. Rock forward vigorously, then back, flexing arms.

Single Knee Circle with Regrip

2. On next forward rock, bend one leg, place it up and over arm on same side. Flex arms as for chin position, thus helping to raise the body.

3. With body raised by momentum of swing, momentarily release the hand, over which the leg is elevated, allowing knee to pass ring.

4. Instantly regrip hand as knee clears ring.

Finish: Return to mat.

Spot on upper arm and small of back.

Variation: To simplify and prepare for the regrip, the simple swing-up should be practiced and should always precede the above stunt. Body swings up, bent leg is placed on arm, but there is no release of grip. This gives the feel of the stunt and helps to develop the necessary timing and coordination.

Further Variations: Execute stunt with other leg and arm; *or* finish in chin position. Drop to mat; *or* execute with straight leg; *or* release both hands as leg passes ring. Follow by landing on mat.

Spot carefully on arm and back for last stunt.

EXERCISES ON THE SWINGING RINGS

With the swing well mastered, the elementary exercises can be executed in the swing; each position to be held for one full swing. At first, the swings should be rather low, increasing in height as skill improves.

Start: Upstart. Swing, with firm grip.

1. On forward swing, thrust legs up, as hips flex.

2. At height of forward swing, assume upstart.

3. Hold for full swing, legs straight, toes pointed.

4. At height of forward swing, legs begin downward swing, body reaching full prone position when passing over the point directly below apparatus suspension.

From the upstart, the following positions can be executed: bird's nest, knee hang, inverted hang, backward hang, sit—all familiar and well mastered. These and other positions developed by the performer can be combined into an impressive routine.

Upstart on Swinging Rings

A   B   C

Bird's Nest on Swinging
Rings

Knee Hang on Swinging
Rings

Inverted Hang on
Swinging Rings

Backward Hang on
Swinging Rings

Sitting Position on Swinging Rings

Start: Upstart, rings within arms' reach.
1. Upstart into knee hang.
2. Whip arms slightly as body is pulled up with abdominal pull, until webbing above rings is grasped.
3. Rise into sit position.
4. Whip legs lightly and rotate backward, flexing hips.
5. Continue rotation until back is fully arched, head up.
6. Hold; legs straight, toes pointed.
7. To return, tuck head tightly to chest as hips flex.

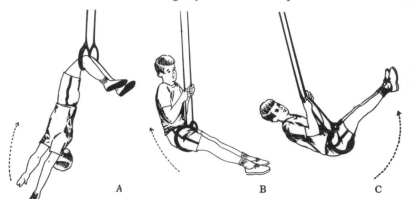

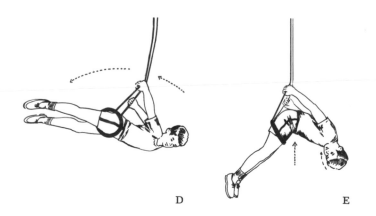

In-Ring Backward Roll and Return

8. Bend arms at elbows, thus assisting in reverse rotation.

Finish: Return to sit; then knee hang, then slow return to
    mat.

Spot standing below and to side of rings, arms ready to
assist if needed.

It is helpful if student thinks of thrusting buttocks to the
ceiling when beginning the return rotation.

DOUBLE BACKWARD CUT-OFF DISMOUNT

Start: Upstart, with legs spread on either side of arms, rings
    just above the head.

1. Make a strong backward rock until visibility is about 20
    feet ahead along the mat.

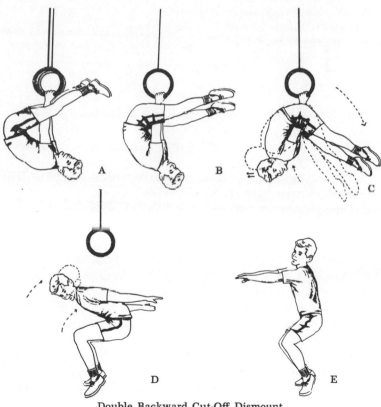

Double Backward Cut-Off Dismount

2. When strong rock is mastered, the spotter should prepare to attend release of grip.
3. At height of backward rock, with long stretch of floor visible, thrust head up. Body rotates backward.
4. Release grip. Snap legs under body and throw shoulders back.

Finish: Land on balls of feet, knees cushioning shock, arms extended forward or out to sides.

Spot on forearm and small of back during rock; on shoulder (or high on upper arm) and leg for dismount. If necessary, another spotter, positioned on opposite side of rings, may assist as needed.

To facilitate learning, the rings may be lowered to allow legs to reach mat before grip release. Student can practice the rock and even land on the mat without releasing his grip— an aid when confidence is needed.

Variation: Single Cut-off Dismount: Execute as above, except that only one leg passes outside the arms, the other passing between arms.

FRONT DISLOCATE

Start: Stand below rings, adjusted just above head.
1. Grasp rings and assume upstart.
2. Thrust hips up. A bounce action is set up and the body gradually gains height.
3. Having developed a good, controlled bounce, thrust legs up and back. Lift head; arch back.
4. Immediately spread arms out to sides, allowing shoulders to rotate free of body weight.

Finish: Return to mat.

Spot under shoulder and on shins, to assist in up-and-over rotation, if needed. As arms spread and body straightens, retain one hand under shoulders and extend other arm, palm up, under thighs. Should student fail to gain sufficient momentum to relieve arms of body weight, this two-arm under-body guard prevents shoulder injury.

NOTE: At this time, it helps to lower rings to shoulder height. The performer should execute backward somersault and practice the shoulder action with feet on mat. (See figure E, p. 89)

Once learned, the dislocate should be executed with rings high enough so toes cannot touch mat.

Variation: Dislocate can be executed on flying rings: this begins with an upstart and occurs at height of a forward or backward swing. First attempts should be in a low swing, with full mat protection the length of the swing.

Spotter stands below performer at point of height of swing.

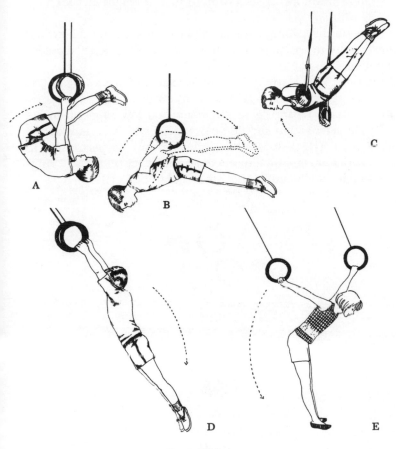

Front Dislocate

INLOCATE

Start: Stand below rings, hands gripping rings just above head.

1. Spotter lifts one leg up as body rotates up and back. Force is gained from push-off of other leg.
2. Reverse the dislocate shoulder rotation as body assumes pike (90-degree angle) position.
3. Head tucked to chest, continue forward rotation until legs land on mat.

Finish: When executed from swing on still rings, finish is downward swing and drop to mat at height of backward swing.

Spot on the leading leg in two places at start; on thighs and lower hips to assist in lift, thus allowing for safe shoulder rotation.

Variation: Well learned, inlocate is executed in a swing on the flying rings, at height of backward swing.

NOTE: Again returning to somersault on low rings, dislocate shoulder action should be practiced with feet on mat.

Variation: The dislocate and inlocate may be performed in series or combined to make performance on the still rings more challenging and spectacular.

Inlocate

Strength Moves—For Boys Only

The following exercises fall into the category of men's gymnastics, since considerable arm strength and powerful abdominal muscles are required. These exercises are excellent for the older boy, eager to advance, provided his strength and skill permit.

Start: Rings high enough to require a strong jump to grasp.
1. Make several strong, high swings.
2. At height of backward swing, bend elbows somewhat, as
   momentum frees arms of body weight.
3. Press arms down hard.
Finish: Straight-arm support.
   Spotter may assist at first by grasping thighs and lifting.
   Timing is important in this exercise.

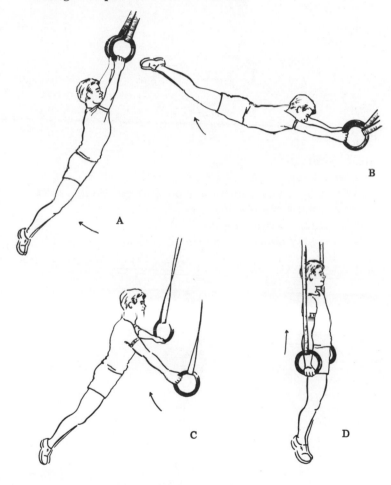

Backward Uprise

Start: Straight-arm support.
1. Slowly raise legs until parallel to floor.
2. Hold; legs rigid, toes pointed, head up.
Finish: Make slow return to straight-arm support.

Half Lever

DIP

Start: Straight-arm support.
1. Lower body slowly, as elbows bend.
2. With elbows bent, at almost 90 degrees. Hold.
3. Straighten arms slowly, as body is elevated.
Finish: Straight-arm support.

Spotter may assist by grasping calves or thighs and lifting, as needed.

Dip

7

❋ ❋ ❋

HORIZONTAL BAR

Any bar within reach fascinates young children. They swing, climb, and sway to and fro on it as they try to master some movement or at least wrap their knees or ankles around it.

The horizontal bar is a simple, yet challenging, piece of apparatus. The first movements outlined are similar to those on the rings. Successive stunts utilize momentum, coupled with timing and centrifugal force. The majority of the maneuvers are done in the tuck position.

There are no strength moves involved here. The purposes of the outlined exercises are pure enjoyment and the development of a good sense of timing and coordination.

If no gym or regulation equipment is available, an outdoor horizontal bar is an excellent substitute (see figure, p. 94). The ideal height of the horizontal bar for children is at the level of the upper chest.

Though horizontal bar stunts may be started in conjunction with other stunts on other apparatus, many children find horizontal bar work easier after mastering the preliminaries on other apparatus. This, of course, will vary with the individual.

Outdoor Horizontal Bar

The horizontal bar should be approximately the height of the upper chest. The ground under, in front of, and behind the bar should be dug up to a depth of 6 inches. The soil should be removed and replaced by sand. This makes a safe padding, better than a mat on a hard surface. To keep the bar smooth, rub it with emery paper or steel wool.

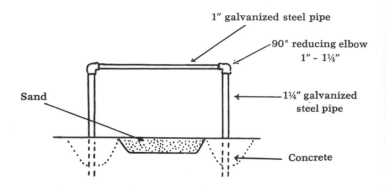

1″ galvanized steel pipe

90° reducing elbow
1″ - 1¼″

Sand

1¼″ galvanized
steel pipe

Concrete

Outdoor Horizontal Bar

ELEMENTARY WORK ON THE HORIZONTAL BAR

These exercises can be performed upon either a standard indoor horizontal bar or on the outdoor bar constructed from galvanized steel pipe, as illustrated above. The bar should be the height of the upper chest.

Regular Grip

1. Facing the bar, place palms over the bar. Curl the fingers down and lock.
2. Curl thumbs under bar, away from the body.

REVERSE GRIP

1. Facing bar, extend arms forward, palms up.
2. Pass hands under the bar and place palms on bar, facing the body.
3. Curl fingers over and around bar, toward the body.
4. Curl thumbs around bar from beneath, toward the body.

Reverse Grip

FRONT-SUPPORT MOUNT

Start: Bar at chest level, hands in regular grip.
1. From stand, flex knees.
2. Jump and push downward with arms.

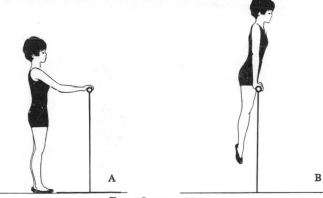

A   B

Front-Support Mount

3. Straighten arms, legs straight, toes pointed.
4. Hold; head up, hips against bar (straight-arm support).
Finish: Push off from bar with arms. Return to mat. Stand.
    a. Toes leading, land on balls of feet.
    b. Bend knees to cushion landing.
Correct form should be mentioned but not required.

Spot using hand-on-hand guard and grasping upper arm. This provides a slight boost when needed. Spotting position is to the side of the performer.

BACKWARD DISMOUNT

Start: Straight-arm support.
1. Make slight forward swing of legs; knees rigid, toes pointed.
2. Swing legs back forcefully.
3. At height of backward swing, flex hips and point toes to mat, retaining grip on bar.
4. Land on mat, on balls of feet, knees cushioning shock.
Finish: Erect stand, arms at sides.
    This is the basis of the dismount and should be well learned.
    Spot as for front-support mount, on hand and upper arm.
Variation: Release hands at height of backward swing, and make an unsupported drop to mat.
    It is best to keep the initial swings low.

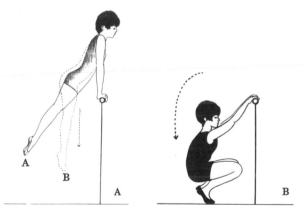

Backward Dismount

Start: Squat beneath bar, hands in regular grip.
1. Kick one leg up as other pushes off mat.
2. Pass both legs under bar, knees bent, as body rotates backward.
3. Having completed a half-circle, land on mat, toes first, hands still gripping bar.

Finish: Release hands from bar. Rise to stand.

Spot on upper arm, legs or back, as needed.

Variation: Begin stunt with double-leg takeoff from mat.

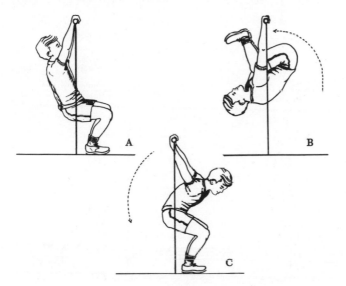

Backward Under-Bar Somersault

FORWARD SOMERSAULT

Start: Straight-arm support, body erect, legs straight.
1. Lean body forward over bar, gradually shifting weight to pelvic area.
2. Weight removed from arms, change to reverse grip.
3. Begin forward rotation as body bends and rolls over bar.
4. Slowly lower body to mat, legs straight.

Finish: Rise to stand.

Spot in front and to side of bar, hand on small of the back, the other on arm.

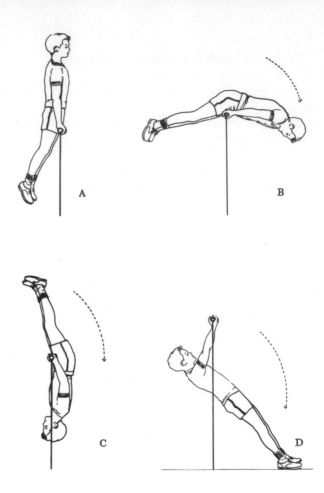

Forward Somersault

BACKWARD SOMERSAULT

Start: Stand, followed by squat before bar, using regular grip.
1. Flex arms. Lead with one leg in kick-off from mat.
2. Push off with other leg, and bend head backward.
3. Flex at hips as body touches and passes over the bar, legs together and straight, toes pointed.
4. End rotation in straight-arm support. Hold.
Finish: Backward dismount, ending in erect stand.

Spot in front of bar, one hand on arm; the other, first on legs, then on small of back as rotation continues.

Some may find the reverse grip easier.

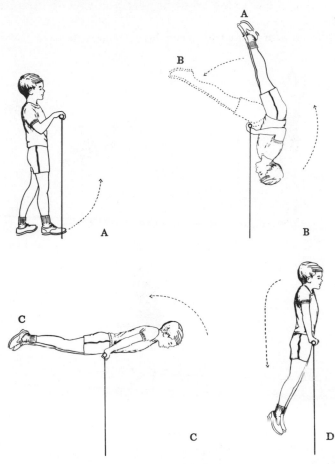

Backward Somersault

FORWARD UNDERSWING

Start: Stand, hands on bar in regular grip.
1. Swing one leg back, then forward.
2. Swing both legs forward, arms flexing.
3. Arch back; legs straight, toes pointed and reaching down.
4. Release grip as toes near mat; head up.

5. Torso moves forward and up when feet touch mat.

Finish: Bend knees to cushion landing. End either in squat or rapid squat-to-stand, arms extended as shown.

At first, a low swing with the feet just leaving the mat is best.

Spot on arm and under shoulders. (Figure A, page 10)

Forward Underswing

UNDER-BAR BACKWARD SOMERSAULT WITH KNEE CATCH

Start: Squat under bar; regular grip.

1. Kick one leg up. Follow with push-off by other leg.
2. Bend knees, rotating body backward until one knee can be bent over the bar, toe pointed.
3. Extend other leg forward under bar.
4. Lean head backward. Arch back, holding extended leg rigid, toes pointed.
5. Hold.

6. Bend extended leg and pass it under bar. Straighten both legs into upstart.
7. Continue backward rotation until feet touch mat.

Finish: Return to squat, then to erect stand.

Variation: Bent legs come to rest under the bar. Next they extend directly up on either side of bar, with the body vertical in inverted hang.

Spot on arm and leg during backward rotation; on arm and instep during hold; on arm and under body, not touching the performer unless necessary.

Henceforth spotting of the upward rotation may be omitted. The motion should have been mastered at this point.

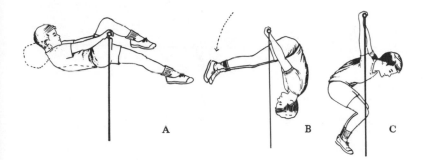

Under-Bar Backward Somersault with Knee Catch

OVER-BAR BODY TURN WITH CROTCH SEAT

Start: Straight-arm support, regular grip.

1. Swing ("Y") leg up over bar (see figure B, p. 102).
2. Turn body a quarter turn into crotch seat.
3. Reverse grip of far hand and move it in front of near hand. Palms now face each other.
4. Return same leg to starting position, or bring other leg back and over bar. (In the latter case, execute a half turn and finish facing in opposite direction.)
5. As leg swings up, hand not supporting body weight regrips bar in regular grip.

Finish: Straight-arm support, followed by drop to mat.
Spot on arm; also on leg if necessary.

Variation: To simplify exercise, swing one leg up and place it momentarily on bar before continuing.

Legs remain straight with pointed toes, back is erect and head is held high.

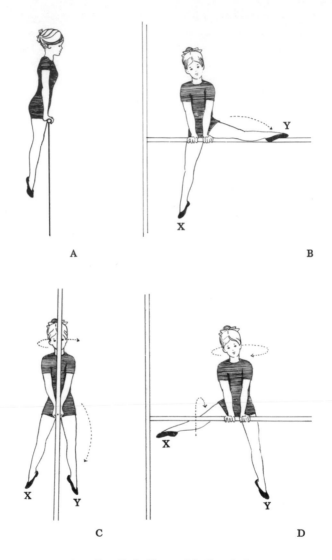

A

B

C

D

Over-Bar Body Turn with Crotch Seat

BACKWARD HALF-CIRCLE WITH LEG EXTENSION

Start: Crotch seat, right hand behind right buttock. Left hand grips bar in front of body.

1. Swing up left leg, weight shifting to right buttock and arm.
2. Release grip on bar with left hand, as left leg clears bar and comes to rest next to right leg.
3. Regrip left hand next to left leg, body now in backward rest.
4. Bend hips as body eases back into a sit, weight supported mostly by arms.
5. Keeping legs rigid, lift them as high as possible, tensing arms to help support body.
6. Hold; back erect, head high, toes pointed.
7. Hips slide back and knees bend as body rotates backward.

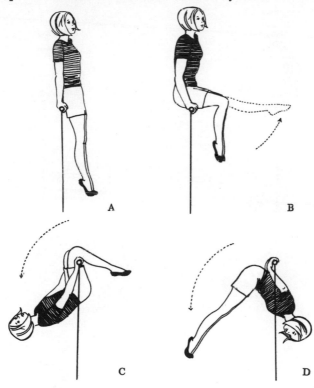

A   B

C   D

Backward Half-Circle with Leg Extension

Finish: Squat, hands still gripping bar. Release grip and stand.

Spot on arm and small of back or shoulders, spotter always to rear of performer.

Variation: Hands are placed together for crotch seat and remain between legs throughout exercise, being released before landing on mat.

As skill increases it is best that the arms bear full body weight during the hold, hips slightly up off bar.

BACKWARD HALF-KNEE CIRCLE WITH ROCK

Start: Straight-arm support.

1. Swing right leg up and over bar, knee rigid, toes pointed.
2. As left arm supports body, clear bar with right leg. Regrip right hand on outside of right leg. This is a straddle rest.

Backward Half-Knee Circle with Rock

3. Bend right knee as body leans back and swings below the bar.
4. Use the momentum gained with the rocking of the torso to set up a good back and forth swing under the bar.

Finish: As body comes to rest, bring both legs under the bar, between the hands and down to mat.

Spot on arms and under torso; also on arm and instep during rocking motion.

This stunt gives the feel of the full knee circle, a more advanced move. Rocking should reach the three-quarter point.

Variation: Entire stunt may be reversed, rotating the body forward.

If there is some reluctance toward the rotation, a hand, placed on the back (in the back rotation) or on the front shoulders (in forward rotation) will aid greatly in giving needed confidence. In these cases, the body is lowered slowly, spotter bearing weight of the body.

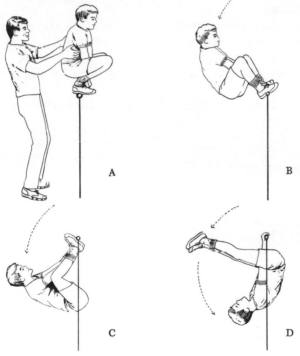

A

B

C

D

Backward Squat Roll

Start: Straight-arm support. (Spotter stands behind performer, guarding waist with both hands.)
1. Assume squat position on bar, hands between legs in regular grip. (Spotter steps to side, grasps one arm and steadies
performer with other hand on back.)
2. Rotate backward.
3. Complete half-circle. When body is upside down, straighten
legs and land on mat.
Finish: Release hands from bar; rise to stand.
Variation: Place hands outside of legs at start of exercise.

BACKWARD SQUAT ROLL WITH FORWARD UNDERSWING

Start: Squat on bar, hands between the legs. (Spotter steps
in front of bar and steadies performer on upper arm and
back.)
1. Rotate body backward. (Spotter releases grip on arm and
squats down, prepared for the underswing guard [figure
A, page 10].)
2. As the feet leave the bar, straighten legs and reach for
the mat.
3. Arch body out and up, as previously learned in the forward
underswing (page 100).

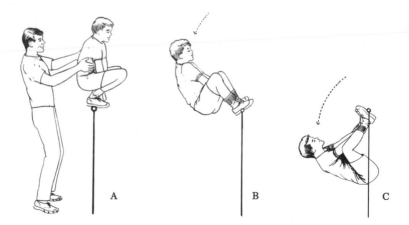

A   B   C

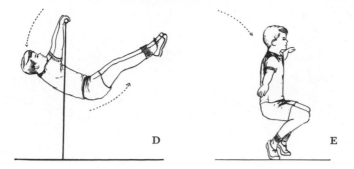

D   E

Backward Squat Roll with Forward Underswing

Finish: Squat landing on mat, arms extended forward or out to sides.

Variation: Execute stunt with legs between the hands; *or* with legs straight and extended out to sides, hands together between legs. As body swings down, let legs leave bar and come together in midst of forward underswing.

This stunt should be carefully guarded until fully mastered.

FORWARD KNEE-REST UNDERSWING

Start: Kneel on bar, hands next to legs, position steadied by spotting on upper arm and above wrist.

(Spotter is forward of bar.)

1. In kneel, arms bear some of body weight; hands in regular grip.
2. With spotter in front of bar, rotate body backward.
3. Releasing grip, spotter squats to guard the underswing which follows.
4. When knees are parallel to mat, let knees leave bar. Extend legs forward and straighten.
5. Arch body out and up, as previously learned in the forward underswing (page 100).

Finish: Squat landing, arms forward or to the sides.

Variation: Place hands between knees at start of exercise.

Forward Knee-Rest Underswing

OVER-BAR SPINE ROLL

Start: Upstart position, hands in regular grip.
1. Straighten body into inverted hang, bar in front of buttocks.
2. Flex hips, whipping legs back slightly, then thrust them smartly forward and over the bar, hips following and adding force.
3. As momentum brings body over the bar, the back arches.
4. By continuing downward thrust of legs, the torso is raised to erect position.
5. Straighten arms fully, helping to support body weight.

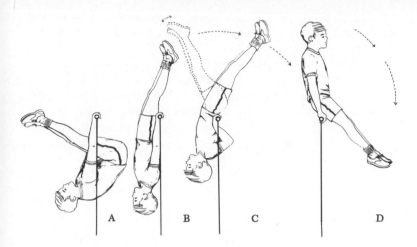

Over-Bar Spine Roll

6. Flex hips and ease buttocks onto bar.

7. Semi-sit on bar.

Finish: Lead into landing on mat with forward swing of both legs and push-off with both arms.

Spot forward and to the side of bar, one hand on upper arm, the other on the legs. As body rolls over the bar the arm guarding the legs is in position to guard the torso at the shoulders to prevent overbalancing.

NOTE: Avoid bearing weight on the spine. As the legs whip over the bar, flex the arms and tense, keeping the spine protected from undue pressure. Keep the legs straight and the toes pointed throughout the exercise.

HIP CIRCLE

Start: Straight-arm support.

1. Swing legs backward, knees straight, toes well pointed.

2. At height of backward swing, bring legs forward forcefully, hips flexing and touching bar.

3. Centrifugal force continues body in backward rotation until a full circle is completed.

Finish: Backward dismount.

Spot forward and to the side of the performer, one hand on

upper arm, the other ready to assist as needed, generally on the legs.

Since the horizontal bar presents less opportunity for simple movements, work upon the bar may move slowly. It is often helpful if other apparatus work with movements similar to horizontal bar work precedes the exercises on the bar. If the movements have been perfected, the performer can concentrate on the important element of timing on the horizontal bar.

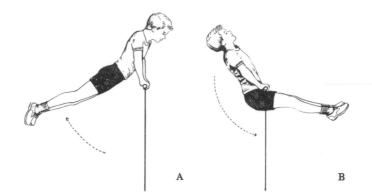

A   B

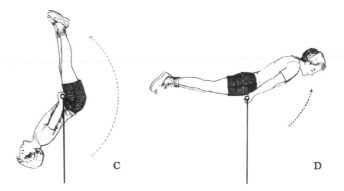

C   D

Hip Circle

INTERMEDIATE WORK ON THE HORIZONTAL BAR

SINGLE KNEE CIRCLE FORWARD

Start: Straddle rest, using reverse grip.

1. Thrust body forward, knee of forward leg bending around the bar.
2. Centrifugal force plus a downward thrust of extended leg and pull-up on arms swings body back into start position.

Finish: Rotate body backward into a hang from one knee. Dismount into squat.

Single Knee Circle Forward

Spot forward of bar, on arm, other hand ready if needed; also on top of extended leg and under shoulders during upward rotation. Should insufficient momentum be gained, the torso can be assisted upward.

It is important that the child should not be afraid when attempting circles. Therefore, mastery of the under-bar rock (page 104) is necessary.

Variation (a modification for the younger child):

    a. End forward thrust in rock.

    b. With a strong downward thrust of extended leg and pull up on arms, swing body up into start position.

Spot forward of bar, one hand under shoulders, other on lower shin of extended leg, assisting with downward leg thrust.

Variation, Single Knee Circle Backward: action reverses, hands in regular grip.

Spot arm and lower shin or instep of bent leg in backward pitch. In upward rotation, spot arm and other hand, ready to catch shoulders and assist in completing circle.

Be sure to have chalk handy for safe, sure grip.

DOUBLE KNEE CIRCLE BACKWARD

Start: Backward rest, using regular grip.

1. Ease into sit on bar.
2. Slide hips back and thrust body backward, knees hooking around bar. Thrust head well to the rear.
3. Centrifugal force, plus continued backward thrust of head and body completes the circle.

Finish: Sit on bar.

Spot in front of bar, holding arm and lower shins during backward rotation. Spot on arm and upper chest, if necessary, during upward rotation.

Variation: Use the rocking motion in conjunction with the full circle.

This is helpful in establishing the feel of the movement. Timing and good coordination are important when circles are performed.

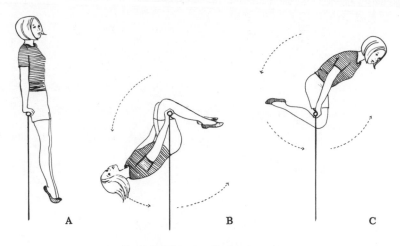

Double Knee Circle Backward

Double Knee Circle Backward with Rock

MILL CIRCLE

Start: Straddle rest, reverse grip.
1. Keeping legs straight, thrust body forward as in single knee circle.
2. With the upper inner thighs the fulcrum, execute a full circle.

Finish: Start position.
  Spot as for knee circle.

Variation: Execute mill circle to the rear, using regular grip.

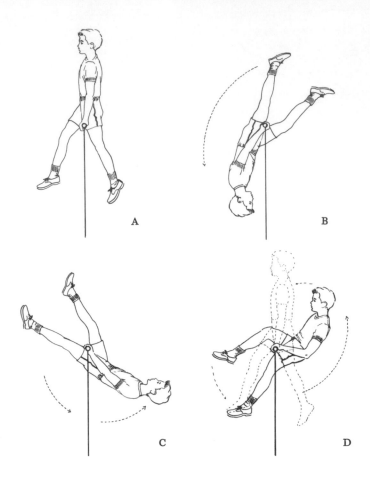

Mill Circle

HOCK CIRCLE

Start: Sit on bar (adjusted to shoulder height).
1. Execute the double knee circle backward.
2. As head and body are thrust backward, release hands and thrust them overhead.
3. Centrifugal force and body thrust return performer to sit on bar.

Spot with care, in front of the bar, on shins; then by following the torso with one hand on small of back, the other on the front shoulders. There should be no actual contact with torso of performer, unless necessary.

This stunt is really a step over the threshold into the advanced class and is for *the skilled only*.

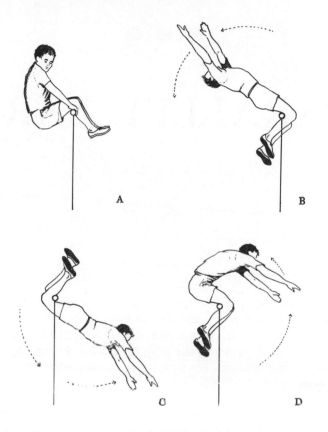

Hock Circle

8

❀ ❀ ❀

PARALLEL BARS

Outdoor Parallel Bars

Since outdoor parallel bars are not adjustable to the size of the performer, it is preferable to have one set for the older children and one for small children. If this is not possible, the bars should be set at shoulder height for the average ten-year-old, and just far enough apart for his shoulders to fit between.

Outdoor parallel bars have limited use for children because the equipment is not adjustable. Only the exercises executed under the bars and a few exercises in the straight-arm-support position can be performed safely. Bruises on arms and legs can result from above-bar work on rigid equipment inappropriate for the child's size.

Outdoor parallel bars can be made of 1¼-inch galvanized steel pipe and 1½-inch pipe, joined with reducing elbows. The ends of the supporting pipe must be embedded in concrete. The ground under and around the installed parallel bars should be dug up to a depth of 6 inches and replaced with sand.

This equipment is safe, stable, easy to construct and in-expensive.

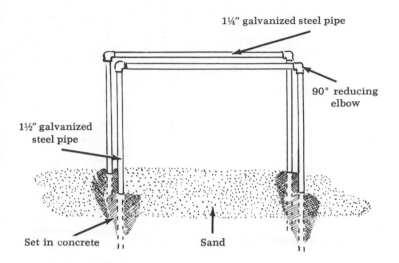

1¼" galvanized steel pipe

90° reducing elbow

1½" galvanized steel pipe

Set in concrete

Sand

Outdoor Parallel Bars

Indoor Parallel Bars

A good set of parallel bars for indoor use is unsurpassed in usefulness and durability by any other item of gymnasium equipment. This precision-built piece of apparatus has two strong, flexible wooden bars with adjustable metal supports. The bars should adjust easily and hold securely in each position.

If the only bars available cannot be lowered sufficiently for use with children, some modification can be made by stacking mats under the bars (see figure, p. 118). When the space between the bars cannot be adjusted properly, do not allow the children to perform above-bar exercises. They can perform under-bar exercises, however, and, through these, develop enough strength in the arms to learn to execute swings and seats. In intermediate parallel bar work, the shoulder stands and other maneuvers in which the support is on the upper arm should be omitted if the bars cannot be adjusted to the child's size.

Indoor Parallel Bars

Indoor Parallel Bars with Stacked Mats

Low Practice Parallel Bars

Practicing handstands and upper-arm stands on the low bars relieves the novice of fear of height.

Practice bars may be easily and inexpensively made from 1-inch galvanized steel pipe and fittings (see figure B, p. 119), with 1-inch wooden dowels for the bars. Tape should be wrapped around the ends of the dowels to insure a tight fit. If the dowel is a bit large it may be shaved down to the required size, wrapped with tape and screwed into place. The wood should be sanded and sealed.

Children and the Parallel Bars

Persons whose only acquaintance with parallel bars is in watching expert gymnasts perform find it difficult to imagine small children performing on this equipment. Immediately questions are raised: Can children master the basics? Will they enjoy this form of activity? Is it dangerous?

No doubt remains, however, in the minds of school or recreation administrators who have observed small children participate in a carefully planned program of activity on the parallel bars. Children actually love it and thrive on it. They can not only master the basics but gain great value from it.

As to safety, by using common sense and the technique of spotting, plus firm observance of basic discipline in the gym, work on the parallel bars can be made safer than riding a bicycle or roller skating. Rules and precautions are fully covered in the chapter on safety.

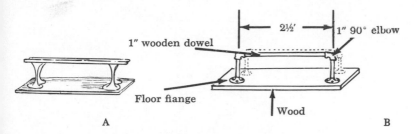

Low Practice Parallel Bars

ELEMENTARY WORK ON THE PARALLEL BARS

GRIP FOR STRAIGHT-ARM SUPPORT

1. Place hands on the bars, from the top.
2. Rest palms on top of the bars, and curl fingers around the outside of each bar.
3. Curl the thumb over the bar on the inside.
   This is called an overhand grip.

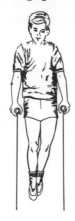

Grip for Straight-Arm Support

1. Grasp bars from beneath.
2. Place palms on the outside of the bars.
3. Curl fingers down over top of bars.
4. Place thumbs on the bar next to palms.

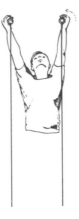

Hanging Grip

ⓑ UNDER-BAR KNEE HANG

Start: Semi-squat position in center of bars set at shoulder
height or slightly lower. Width of bars should be equal to
width of shoulders.
1. Grip bars from outside, palms facing each other.
2. Kick up with one leg, followed by push-off with other leg.
3. Hook knees over the bars from inside.

A   B

C

Under-Bar Knee Hang

4. Hold, toes pointed, head leaned back.

Finish: Make slow return to mat.

Spot on small of back and upper arm; or, for the younger child, on the hand and leg during ascent, and on hand and small of back in full position.

UPSTART

Start: Semi-squat in center of bars; bars at shoulder height or slightly lower.

1. Grip bars from outside, palms facing each other.
2. Kick up with one leg, followed by push-off with other leg.
3. Rotate body backward, and straighten legs.
4. When legs are extended above the torso and the point of balance for this position is reached, backward rotation ends.

Upstart

5. Hold; legs straight, toes pointed.

Finish: Make slow return to mat.

Spot on upper arm and small of back, on hand and leg, then on hand and back in full position for the small child.

A hard rebound of the legs to the mat should be avoided and a slow, controlled descent achieved. Flexing the arms and at the same time using abdominal muscles are required for a slow descent. It is important that this be mastered. It is helpful for the spotter to place one hand on the small of the back of the performer.

Movements Beginning with the Upstart

A. INVERTED HANG

1. From upstart, slowly straighten body, extending legs upward.
2. Body perpendicular to mat, arch head back, holding legs straight, toes pointed. Arch the back sufficiently to achieve balance.

Finish: Return to upstart and make slow return to mat.

Spot on arm and legs.

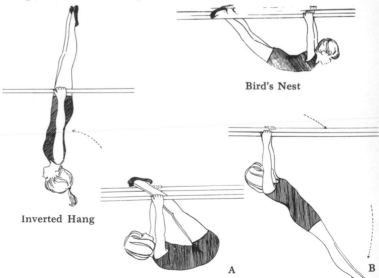

Bird's Nest

Inverted Hang

A

B

Descent from Parallel Bars

1. Continue backward rotation of body until insteps touch top of bars.
2. Slide insteps along bars until back is fully arched and body extended, head raised.
3. Hold for several seconds.
4. Tuck head to chest and flex hips to reverse the rotation.

Finish: Return to upstart and make slow return to mat.

Spot on arm and back as backward rotation occurs; on arm and under abdomen in full position.

BACKWARD SOMERSAULT

Start: Squat position in center of bars.
1. Kick up to upstart, legs straight, toes pointed.
2. Continue backward rotation until balls of feet touch mat.

Finish: Release grip; rise to stand, arms at sides.

Spot on arms and back. The hand-on-hand technique should no longer be required and a grip on the arm should be used instead.

Backward Somersault

Variation: To simplify, keep knees bent throughout stunt; *or* for more challenge, reverse entire exercise, starting from position 2 above. Flex knees and, with a double-leg push-off, rotate forward.

At this time it is good to learn how to approach the aparatus to give the entire performance a polished, well-executed appearance. The walk to and from all apparatus should be executed with a squaring of corners. There should also be a stand of several seconds in the attention position (erect stand, head up, and arms at sides), both before and after apparatus is used.

The following movements should be preceded by conditioning exercises, such as chin-ups on the rings or floor push-ups. Many youngsters lack the muscle strength in the arms necessary for straight-arm-support exercises. A fall between the bars can be painful and discouraging.

③ STRAIGHT-ARM WALK

Start: Approach bars from one end.

1. Grip bars in overhand grip. (See figure on page 119)
2. Make a strong jump and press downward with arms into straight-arm support. This should be practiced until it becomes easy.
3. Keeping legs straight and toes pointed, sway body from side to side.

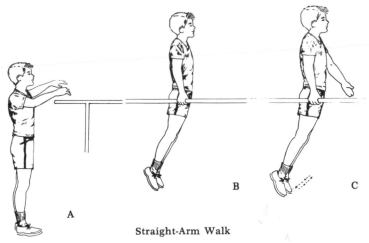

B   C

A

Straight-Arm Walk

4. After a few preliminary sways, sway legs to the right. Move right hand forward an inch or two. (Torso leans to the left, and left arm momentarily supports body weight.)
5. As weight shifts from side to side, the hands "walk" along the bars.

Finish: Stop motion. Drop to mat, lowering arms to sides.

Spot on one arm in two places for older children, spotter to one side of bars; spot on the waist for younger children, spotter standing behind child.

Variation: Backward walk.

It is important that bars be adjusted to the width of the shoulders and that very short "steps" are taken with the hands. Trying to move the hands too far along the bars with each movement can result in loss of balance and a fall forward.

STRAIGHT-ARM SWING

Start: Straight-arm support at center of apparatus.
1. With both legs straight and toes pointed, swing forward, then back.
2. Continue swinging until several full swings have been completed.
3. Stop all motion. Drop to mat, arms at sides.

Finish: Stand at attention and march away from bars.

Spot on the forearm and upper arm, spotter on one side of apparatus.

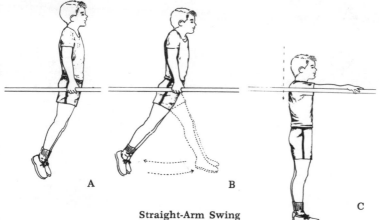

A   B

Straight-Arm Swing

C

This is a basic skill and should be well mastered. The over-enthusiastic beginner should be well guarded. At first, swings should be low, increasing in height, as skill and strength develop. Too high a swing can result in loss of balance and a fall.

⑤ ⟨S T R A D D L E S E A T⟩

Start: Straight-arm swing at center of apparatus.

1. Swing forward, then back, legs straight, toes pointed.
2. On next forward swing, swing legs above level of bars; spread legs and land with thighs on top of bars.
3. Keep hands behind buttocks as body rises forward and up, until body weight is borne on the inner thighs.

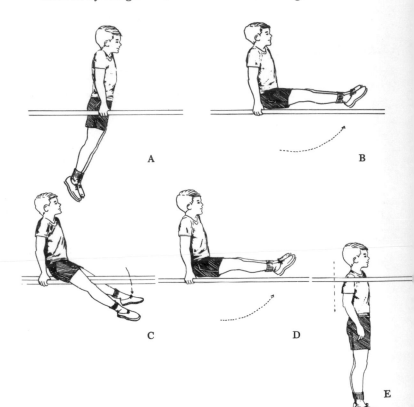

Straddle Seat

Finish: Place arms behind buttocks, swing legs up as arms bear body weight. Return to straight-arm support and drop to mat.

Spot on the forearm and upper arm, spotter at side.

Once exercise is mastered, several swings precede drop to mat, which is executed at height of backward swing. (See figures on page 96)

DISMOUNT FROM RIDING SEAT WITH ⑧ QUARTER TURN

Start: Swing, in straight-arm support, at center of bars.
1. As both legs swing forward, cast them over the bar on the side toward the spotter.
2. Straighten outer leg, extending it downward with toes pointed.
3. Bend inner leg at knee and hip, pointing toes downward. Body weight is now borne by buttock and thigh of bent leg.

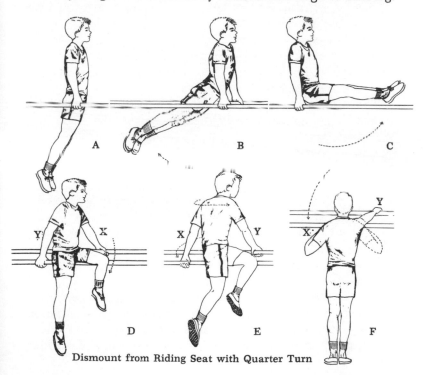

Dismount from Riding Seat with Quarter Turn

4. Retain grip on bars, arch back, holding head high.
5. Hold. When body is correctly positioned, balance is perfect.
6. Arms may now be extended out to the sides. Hold.

Finish: Return arms to bars and reverse movements, ending with drop to mat.

When exercise is well learned, student can continue on to Quarter-Turn Dismount.

QUARTER-TURN DISMOUNT

Start: Grip both bars, far hand on far bar, other hand behind buttock.
1. Reverse positions of hands, far hand behind buttock, near hand on far bar.
2. Shift weight momentarily to arms, as near leg swings forward and thigh of inner leg pushes off near bar.
3. Make a quarter turn of the body just before feet touch mat.
4. Hand on near bar retains its grip; other hand releases but regrips on near bar to complete dismount; grip on both bars may be retained.

Finish: Stand at attention.

Spot two places on the arm, spotter standing at side where riding seat will be executed. The dismount may be spotted at the waist if necessary.

The correct way to land on the mat from any jump dismount has been fully covered in comments on other apparatus activities. (See figures page 96)

Variation: When the above exercise is thoroughly mastered, try the following.
    a. Reverse positions of hands, as for dismount.
    b. Swing outer leg, fully extended, up and over both bars.
    c. Pivot body on thigh of inner leg, knee remaining somewhat less bent, arms bearing much of body weight.

Finish: Straddle seat, facing opposite direction, performer having completed a half turn.

Spot on arm and shoulder if necessary.

All actions should be slow and deliberate and performed with control. Fast movements are difficult to spot and do not develop the muscular tension habits which contribute to safety and proficiency. Speed will come with skill and practice.

Start: Stand, in center of apparatus between the bars. (Bars must be adjusted to width of shoulders.)

1. Place forearms on the bars, elbows bent and fingers curling outward over bars, thumbs curling inward.
2. With grip firm, slowly shift body weight to the forearms, *easing* the body off mat. (If bars are too high to ease up, a small jump may be necessary.)
3. Now, in the forearm support, bear weight on the muscle just below and inward of forearm, where it joins elbow.
4. Both legs held straight, with toes pointed, swing forward, then back, starting a controlled swing.

A   B   C   D

Swing in Forearm Support

Finish: Stop all motion. Drop to mat.

Spot on waist, spotter to side of bars.

Even when correctly performed, the forearm support often produces a bruise on the forearm, just below and inward of the elbow. This is caused by lack of muscle development in this area. Another cause is failure to adjust bars to shoulder width, which makes the bone rather than the muscle take the lion's share of body weight. Therefore, it is most important to check the width adjustment before teaching this exercise.

Variation: A circular swing of legs may replace the back-and-forth swing, movement being limited to the lower torso.

REAR VAULT DISMOUNT

Start: Strong swing in center of apparatus, straight-arm support. (This exercise requires careful spotting.)

1. With legs kept together, at the height of the forward swing, pass both body and legs over the right bar.
2. Back well arched, reach for the mat with the toes. Push off from the bars with both arms.
3. Release the hand on near bar with arm extended to the side; with other hand release grip on far bar and immediately regrip near bar. Retain grip until finish.

Finish: Land on mat, toes leading, knees bending to cushion shock, head up.

Spot on near arm and with extended arm under shoulders.

See pages 9 and 10 for detailed explanation.

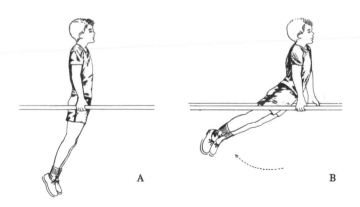

A   B

C

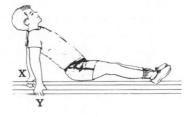

D

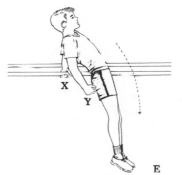

E

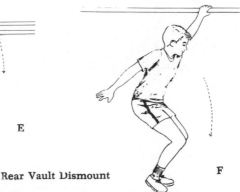

Rear Vault Dismount

F

SWING IN UPPER-ARM HANG

Start: Stand between bars, arms along top of bars adjusted to shoulder width.

1. Bend elbows slightly, curl hands around outside of bars, thumbs on inner side of bars.
2. *Ease* body weight up and onto the upper arms; forearms steady the arms, muscle of upper arm bearing the weight.
3. Begin low swing, legs straight, toes pointed.
4. Stop motion.

Finish: Drop to mat.

Spot at waist when necessary.

Variation: At end of bars, execute a jump into upper-arm support. Dismount at height of backward swing, hips flexed, then drop to mat.

Wooden bars flex under pressure and will not cause

bruises if muscles are developed sufficiently. Metal bars are rigid and, therefore, are not suitable for this exercise.

Variation: On a strong forward swing, assume the upstart position; the result—upstart with upper-arm support.

Variation: To simplify, make a side-to-side swing in this upper-arm support.

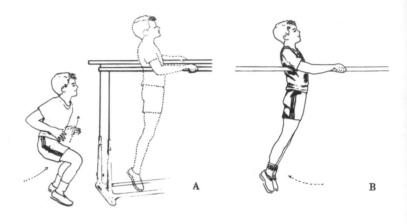

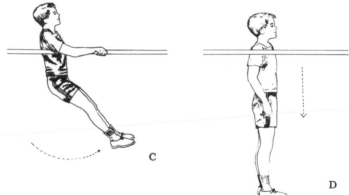

Swing in Upper-Arm Hang

SWING FROM STRADDLE SEAT TO RIDING-SEAT DISMOUNT

Start: Straight-arm swing into straddle seat.

1. In straddle seat, bring hands from behind buttocks and place them forward of thighs.

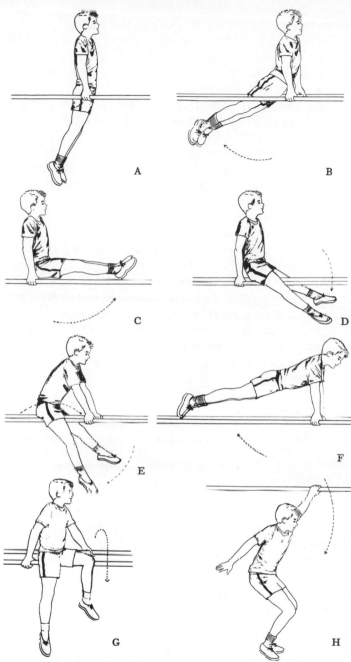

Swing from Straddle Seat to Riding-Seat Dismount

2. Shift body weight to arms, as legs swing smartly backward.
3. When legs clear bars, bring them together and swing them forward and over one bar, ending in riding seat.
4. Swing outside leg forward and out, as arms and thigh of inside leg push off from bars.

Finish: Release far hand grip on far bar and regrip near bar; extend other arm out to side.

Spot on arm and torso as necessary.

Variation: Front Dismount

Instead of swinging into riding seat, keep legs together and swing back again, this time well above the bars at height of backward swing.

    a. Shift weight over right bar as arms assist in pushing off to the right.
    b. When body passes over the right bar, left hand grasps this bar slightly forward of the right hand.
    c. As body descends toward mat, release right-hand grip, retaining grip with left hand until end of dismount.

Finish: Land on mat, right arm extended out to the side.

Spot on right side of bars and forward of performer; also on arms and torso if needed.

Variation: Execute the above exercise to the left, rather than to the right.

SWING IN AND OUT OF STRADDLE SEAT TO RIDING-SEAT DISMOUNT

Start: Straight-arm swing at center of apparatus.
1. Swing legs backward, clearing bars well. At height of backward swing, spread legs out to the sides.
2. As forward motion begins, land legs on either side of the bars, shifting weight to the inner thighs.
3. Move hands behind the buttocks.
4. Whip legs backward, then smartly forward, shifting weight to both arms.
5. Swing legs forward; clear bars, and bring legs together as backward swing begins, thus leading into another forward swing.
6. At height of forward swing, pass both legs over one bar and assume the riding seat.

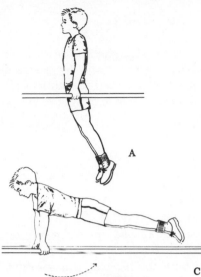

A

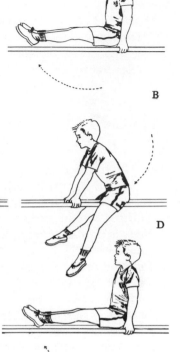

B

C

D

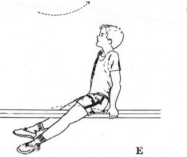

E

F

G

H

Swing in and out of Straddle Seat to Riding-Seat Dismount

135

Finish: Drop to mat as previously learned.

Spot on arm in two places.

Variation: Execute a series of in-and-out straddle seats from one end of bars to the other. Dismount may be executed from end of apparatus on a forward swing, with legs together, as in the forward-swing dismount on the rings. (See figures on pages 130, 131)

FORWARD SOMERSAULT DISMOUNT FROM RIDING SEAT

Start: Riding seat at center of apparatus.

1. Grasp far bar with both hands, as body pivots a quarter turn on the thigh of bent leg.
2. Shifting weight to front of both thighs, hold legs straight. Body is now in forward lean, arms straight and supporting torso.
3. Bending arms, slowly lower body to bars.
4. Change grip to a reverse grip, fingers curling to the rear and around bar, palms to the front.
5. Lean body forward and ease it over the bars. Slowly execute a somersault over the bar forward of the body.

Finish: Slow descent to mat, legs straight, toes pointed.

Spot on arm in two places and on small of back during somersault if necessary. (Spotter should squat and reach under bars.) At this point, very little, if any, contact with the body should be necessary.

Variation:

Start: Forward Lean

    a. Alternately raise legs out to the side and bring them up and over bar supporting legs.

    b. Alternately swing each leg between the bars as far toward the opposite leg as possible, and return.

    c. Execute somersault dismount.

Variation: Alternately extend legs out to the side just above and parallel to bars. Hold; return.

Once these basic moves and combinations are mastered the student can invent moves and combinations all his own. It should be remembered that not all children will advance this far, while others will beg for greater challenge. Each student should be handled according to his interests and physical aptitudes.

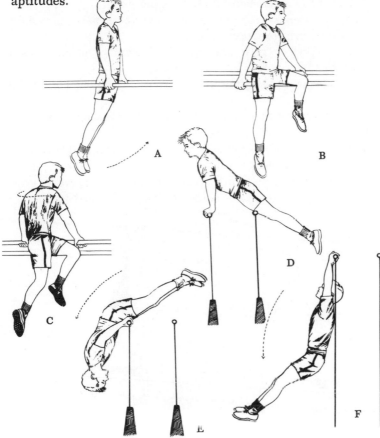

Forward Somersault Dismount from Riding Seat

INTERMEDIATE WORK ON THE PARALLEL BARS

SINGLE-LEG FLANK DISMOUNT

Start: Straddle seat.
1. Make a quarter turn of the body to one side.
2. Hook forward knee around forward bar.
3. Extend rear leg backward, upper thigh on rear bar.

137

4. Grasp forward bar with hand on side of bent leg, palm facing forward; extend other arm out to side.
5. Hold; body erect, head high, toes pointed.
6. Sweep extended rear leg up and over both bars, as weight shifts to arm on forward bar.
7. Retain grip on near bar as body descends and executes a quarter turn before landing on mat.

Finish: Make a neat landing, free arm extended out to the side.

Spot in front and to side of arm grasping bar on upper arm and forearm.

Variation: Execute exercise to other side. A full half-turn may be added to dismount.

Variation: With both hands, grasp forward bar in reverse grip. Follow with one-knee somersault over forward bar.

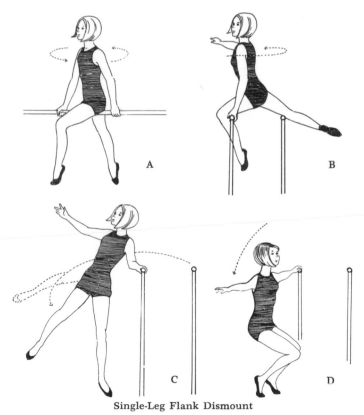

Single-Leg Flank Dismount

Start: Straddle seat at center of apparatus.
1. Grip bars in front of thighs with both hands.
2. Slowly lean body forward, bending elbows until the muscles of the upper arms touch bars.
3. Ease body weight onto upper arms, raising legs up off bars.
4. Torso becomes perpendicular to bars but hips remain flexed and legs spread.
5. Brings legs together slowly and extend them upward.
6. Hold; legs straight, toes pointed.

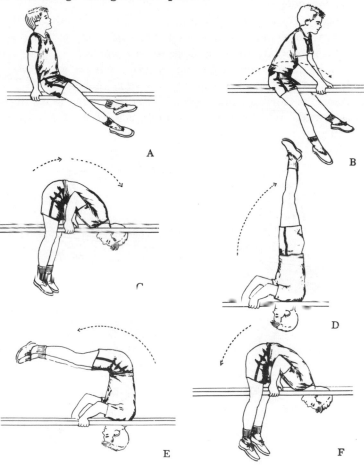

A

B

C

D

E

F

Upper-Arm Stand

7. Slowly reverse the ascent.

Finish: Straddle seat.

Spot on forearm and small of back.

At no time should the shoulders bear body weight. Care must be taken to adjust bars to the width of the shoulders. If bars are too far apart, the upper-arm stand cannot be safely or correctly performed.

FORWARD ROLL

Start: Straddle seat.

1. Begin as for upper-arm stand.
2. From flexed-hip position, body perpendicular to bars, begin to roll body forward; legs remain spread.
3. Rolling on muscle of the upper arm, release grip; rotate forward, and quickly regrasp bars next to hips.
4. Continue forward roll. Arms, next to body, grasp bars somewhat to the inside, forming a surface for hips to roll on.

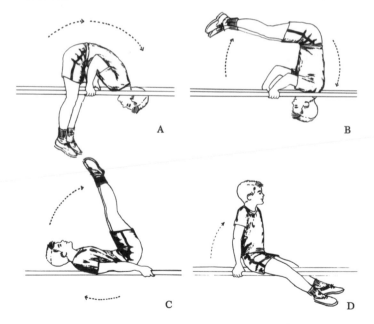

A B C D

Forward Roll

Finish: Straddle rest, hands behind buttocks.

Spot on arm and back up to three-quarters point of rotation; under back thereafter with both hands.

Variation: Reverse entire roll, starting by leaning back and resting shoulders and upper arms on bars, arms in upper-arm hang position. With spread legs, roll body backward on upper-arm muscles. Regrip forward of shoulders, elbows bent. Continue roll and end in straddle seat, grip forward of thighs. (This is the backward straddle shoulder roll.)

ACROSS-BAR REAR SHOULDER STAND

Start: Sit on forward bar; or mount from below the bars.
1. Below-bar mount:
    a. Stand facing length of bars, as both hands grasp nearest bar.
    b. Kick up legs and hook knees over forward bar.
    c. Place one arm at a time on rear bar; grip in upper-arm support fashion.
    d. Arms in this position, straighten legs as hips slide onto forward bar into a layout position across both bars.
2. From sit, hands gripping rear bar, execute slow recline into layout over both bars. Assume grip for upper-arm support.
3. Shift weight to rear of shoulders and hips. Bring both arms forward and grasp forward bar with regular grip.
4. Slowly elevate legs and bend hips as a backward rotation is executed.
5. Maintain pike position until torso is perpendicular to bars.
6. Slowly straighten legs into shoulder stand.
7. Hold; legs straight, toes pointed.
Finish: Return to layout; then into sit or reversal of below-bar-mount movement.
Variation: Spread legs into a split instead of extending them upward; or in full stand position, bend one leg at knee and place sole of that foot on knee of other leg.

Spot at rear bar, on shoulder and back.

Bars must be adjusted to the width of the shoulders. If bars are too far apart, a fall between the bars can occur.

Across-Bar Rear Shoulder Stand

CHEST STAND

Start: Front support at side of one bar.

1. Lean body forward slowly until upper chest rests on forward bar (front lying support).
2. With both hands, regrasp rear bar in reverse grip, *over* the rear bar.
3. Kick up both legs until full balance position is reached.
4. Hold; head up, back well arched, legs straight, toes pointed.

Finish: Make slow descent to front lying support across bars and front straight-arm support.

Spot in front of forward bar on one arm and back or on one arm and legs, as required.

Bars must be adjusted to width of shoulders for safety and ease of performance.

Variation: Chest-Stand Arch-Over. From full chest stand, continue forward rotation of body. As body arches over toward mat, regrip both hands on front bar, using same grip. Both legs land on mat, and grip on forward bar is retained until landing is complete.

Spot on upper arm and back.

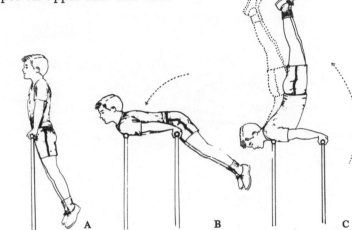

A   B   C

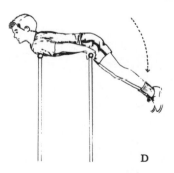   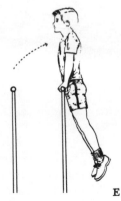

D   E

Chest Stand

TOP UPRISE TO STRADDLE SEAT

Start: Swing, in upper-arm support.

1. At height of strong forward swing, bend hips in pike position above the bars.
2. Quickly roll hips forward with a strong forward, then downward, thrust of outspread legs.
3. As legs near bars, exert strong downward pressure with arms.
4. Body rises as legs touch bars.

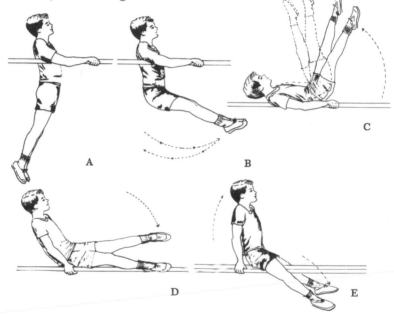

Top Uprise to Straddle Seat

Finish: Straddle seat.

Spot on upper arm and rear shoulders.

Variation: As straddle seat is executed, motion continues:

    a. Lean body forward; weight on inner thighs, swing legs back, regrip hands in front of thighs.

    b. Continue backward swing, arms bearing weight as legs clear bars. Bring legs together and swing them between the bars. This ending is a swing in straight-arm support.

All these movements can be continued into others. It is in this area that a fertile imagination can compose routines which bring gasps and applause from spectators. Often a combination of less difficult moves appears more impressive than a single, difficult stunt.

For Older Boys Only

DIP

Start: Straight-arm support between bars.
1. Slowly and with full control bend arms until almost a 90 degree angle is formed.
2. Hold.
3. Bring body up with strong downward pressure of arms; straighten arms.
Finish: Straight-arm support.
Variation: Dip can be combined with "walk" of hands along the bars, inserting a dip after each forward move of a hand.

Dip

BACKWARD UPRISE

Start: Upper-arm support, bars several inches above shoulders.
1. Make several strong swings to gain momentum.
2. At height of forward swing, bend hips above bars in pike position.
3. Quickly thrust hips and legs forward and down.
4. Momentum of the strong backward swing momentarily

frees the arms of much of body weight. Push arms down hard.

5. Arm pressure brings performer into straight-arm-support swing between the bars.

Finish: Dismount of any type, or landing on bars in riding seat, straddle seat, etc.

Spot on upper arm and under thighs or hips during backward swing to give added lift, if needed.

Once these stunts are mastered, an excellent foundation for continuing into men's or women's events has been established. Performance on apparatus can, in years to come, provide enjoyment and relaxation while building or maintaining strong, attractive bodies. Colleges welcome those skilled in gymnastics, as early training in this sport is rather rare.

Backward Uprise

A   B   C   D   E

9

❀ ❀ ❀

UNEVEN PARALLEL BARS FOR GIRLS

Once girls have thoroughly learned the basics on the even parallel bars, some of the most breathtaking and graceful movements in all gymnastics can be performed on the versatile uneven parallel bars. If the school has purchased quality parallel bars, one bar can be raised to about 7½ feet. This is the maximum height necessary for uneven parallel bar work. The low bar should be slightly below the level of the chin and the upper bar so adjusted that, when one arm is in a forearm support on the low bar, the other hand can easily grasp the high bar.

The exercises stress timing, agility, and balance, and are specifically designed to develop the ideal female form. Because of the height involved in work on the upper bar, it is vital that a good basic background in even-bar work precede the use of this apparatus. It is exceedingly difficult to guard at such a height. This is not an activity for the very young.

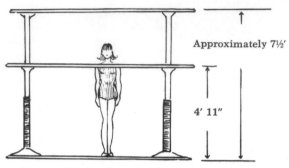

Approximately 7½'

4' 11"

Uneven Parallel Bars for Girls

Basic Exercises

STRAIGHT-ARM SUPPORT

Start: Short run-in and double-leg takeoff from the beatboard.
    (See figures A, B, C, p. 186)
1. With both hands grasp low bar in regular grip.
2. Push down with arms as legs push off from beatboard.
3. Straighten arms and rest thighs against bar.
4. Hold; legs straight, toes pointed, head up.
Finish: Advance to other movements.
    Spotting should not be required in the basic movements,

Straight-Arm Support

148

since even-parallel-bar work must precede any work on the uneven bars.

If bars are lowered for learning stages, it will not be necessary to use a beatboard.

Crotch Seat

CROTCH SEAT

Start: Straight-arm support on low bar.

1. Swing one leg over low bar, as body executes a quarter turn.
2. With hand on side toward high bar, grasp high bar with overhand grip (thumb curled under bar, other hand in front of body).
3. Extend legs down and to the sides, toes pointed, knees rigid.
4. Hold.

Finish: Return to straight-arm support; or lead into next stunt.

Spot on arm and back if necessary.

Variation: Execute stunt with other leg and turn to opposite side.

Start: Crotch seat.

1. Swing leg on side toward high bar up and over low bar.
2. Make a quarter turn with body as hand on low bar regrips next to body.

Finish: Drop to mat; or proceed to next movement.

Spot on torso if necessary.

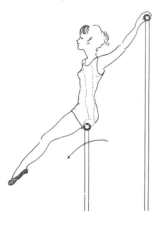

Cross Seat

FORWARD DISMOUNT

Start: Sit on low bar (beatboard removed), both hands gripping low bar.

1. Swing both legs forward simultaneously.
2. Using arms, push off from bar.
3. Extend toes toward mat, as back arches.
4. Land on balls of feet, bending knees to cushion landing.

Finish: Extend both arms to sides or forward.

Spot forward of low bar, on arm, ready to extend arm under shoulders to prevent downward rotation of head and shoulders.

This type of dismount should already be well mastered, having been covered in the exercises on the rings and on the even parallel bars.

Variation: May be begun from crotch seat.

a. Leg between bars swings up and over low bar.

150

b. Now in cross seat, grasp low bar with both hands.
c. Finish as above.

Forward Dismount

BETWEEN-BAR SWING—LOW

Start: Stand between bars, facing open end of apparatus.
1. With one hand, grip low bar in regular grip.
2. Reach other arms up to high bar, palm toward bar.

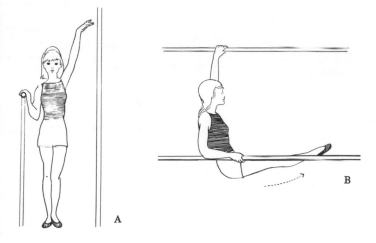

A   B

Between-Bar Swing—Low

3. Make a strong jump to grasp high bar; grip the low bar as for forearm support.
4. Swing both legs forward and back a number of times.
Finish: Stop motion and drop to mat.

   Spot on upper arm, gripping low bar, if necessary.

RIDING SEAT

Start: Swing between bars (no beatboard).
1. On forward swing, sweep both legs over low bar, one arm pulling up, the other pressing down.
2. Extend outer leg downward and bend inner leg; weight is on the inner buttock and thigh.
3. Retain grip. Hold, back arched, head up.
Finish: Reverse action; swing legs up over low bar. Stop action. Drop to mat between bars.

   Spot on arm gripping low bar, if necessary.
Variation: Landing on low bar can be in crotch seat.
   a. Regrip hand on low bar forward of legs.
   b. Swing both legs back and between bars; or swing legs back over low bar, away from apparatus and land on mat. Shift grip on high bar to low bar as body drops; release after landing.

Riding Seat

Variation: From riding seat swing legs forward and away from low bar.
  a. Push off with arm on low bar and release grip.
  b. For landing, regrip low bar with hand from high bar.

QUARTER-TURN BACK DISMOUNT

Start: Riding seat (no beatboard).
1. With rear hand, regrip forward of bent knee.
2. Turn body a quarter turn, as legs push off; with other hand, regrip low bar.
3. Land on both feet, both hands gripping low bar.
Finish: Stand, arms at sides.
  Spot on one arm, if necessary.
The basic mounts and dismounts should be well learned. The beatboard is used only for mounts and should be removed, once apparatus has been mounted.
Variation: For dismount, swing both legs back and down, omitting the quarter turn. This is executed much as is the back dismount on the horizontal bar.

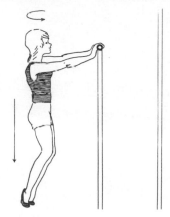

Quarter-Turn Back Dismount

HANG AND SHOOT OVER LOW BAR

Start: Stand under high bar, facing low bar.
1. Bend both legs and push off. With both hands, grasp high bar in regular grip.

2. Body hangs, legs straight, toes pointed, back erect.
3. Swing legs back, then up and over low bar.
4. Land on upper thighs.
5. Bend elbows to allow a recline into a semi-sit.
Finish: Cross seat, followed by forward dismount. (See top figure, p. 151)

Spot forward of low bar, as needed.

Variation: Dismount may be knee hang, followed by backward somersault under low bar.
   a. Slide hips back along low bar, up to knees.
   b. Hook knees around low bar as both hands regrip on low bar and body drops down into knee hang.
   c. Return to mat may be via backward somersault or with forward rotation of straightened legs to mat.
Variation: Flex arms and pull up. Lift legs from low bar; spread and swing backward. Return body to hang from the high bar. Drop to mat.

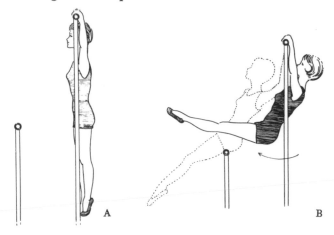

Hang and Shoot over Low Bar

SHOOT-OVER DISMOUNT

Start: Hang on high bar.
1. Swing legs back, then forcefully forward.
2. Pull up with arms as elbows bend.
3. Body shoots up and over low bar, clearing it well.
Finish: Land on mat, toes leading.

Spot forward of low bar, under shoulders.

This dismount is executed as is the forward-swing dismount (see figure, p. 151).

Shoot-over Dismount

BETWEEN-BAR SWING — HIGH

Start: Riding seat or other body support on low bar.
1. Arm on low bar is in straight-arm support; other arm grasps the high bar in a forearm-grip support.
2. Kick legs forward, beginning a swing in this position.
Finish: Stop all motion. Drop to mat, hand on low bar retaining grip. Spot on arm gripping low bar and on torso, if necessary.

This grip should be comfortable. If the grip cannot be made comfortable by lowering the high bar, it may be that the bars should be adjusted inward.

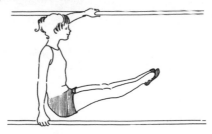

Between-Bar Swing—High

Start: Between-bars swing—high (just learned).

1. On forward swing, cast both legs up and over low bar.
2. Turn body a quarter turn; hand on high bar pushes off and releases as turn begins.
3. Grip low bar with hand from high bar as turn is completed.
4. Push off low bar with both hands, as a forward dismount is executed (see figure, p. 151).

Finish: Land on mat, arms extended forward or out to the sides.

Spot forward of low bar, on arm and back.

Variation: Execute with swing in opposite direction.

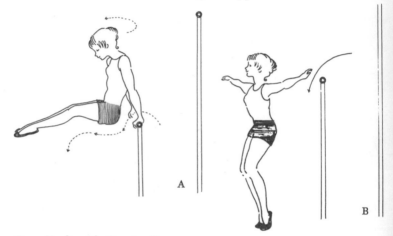

Rear Vault with Quarter Turn

DOUBLE-LEG BOUNCE TO SWAN SUPPORT

Start: Hang on high bar; regular grip.

1. Swing legs back, then up onto low bar; land on calves.
2. Straight legs bounce several times on bar, gaining height.
3. On a good rebound, flex arms and pull up as hips flex; the pull of abdominal muscles brings legs up and over high bar.
4. Straighten arms and assume straight-arm support.
5. Lean body slowly forward, arms supporting body weight.
6. Ease weight gently onto the region just below the pelvic bones.

7. When perfect balance is achieved, extend arms slowly out to the sides, palms down. Keep legs straight.

8. Hold; toes pointed, head up, back arched in balance.

Finish: Return to straight-arm support.

Spot on arm and back during backward rotation. Since the performer should not be touched while in the balance, it is most important that she shall have acquired sufficient skill from elementary and intermediate work on the even parallel bars.

Variation: To gain experience in the swan balance:

a. Straight-arm support on low bar.

b. Lean into swan support.

c. Return to straight-arm support and drop to mat.

Spot under thighs and on one shoulder.

Variation: As body rotates upward, one leg shoots through arms. The swing-up ends with leg held forward and above high bar, other leg extended downward behind high bar. This is a single-leg swing-up.

a. Finish may be forward knee somersault, legs landing gently on low bar, *or*

b. One-knee hang from high bar, followed by hang and drop to mat.

Variation: From single-leg swing-up:

a. Ease leg over and in front of high bar onto low bar.

b. Sweep arm on same side up, palm facing either toward or away from body.

c. With other hand maintain grip on high bar.

d. Extend rear leg straight back, holding head high.

Finish: Regrip extended hand on high bar, both hands in reverse grip. Rotate body forward. Bend both legs, then straighten into the upstart, followed by hang and drop to mat.

Variation: From single-leg swing-up:

a. Hand on outer side of thigh over bar regrips next to the other hand.

b. Rear leg swings up and over bar. Body assumes straddle seat. Arms support body as legs spread and rise up off the bar. (See figures, p. 182)

It is wise to master this on the low bar. Spotter can steady the performer by grasping the waist from behind. Spotter stands below the high bar, with hand ready to assist when performer is on high bar. The need for a good background in apparatus work can be readily recognized. The high bar is no place to falter!

Double-Leg Bounce to Swan Support

UNDERSWING DISMOUNT FROM HIGH BAR

Start: Stand on low bar, hands gripping high bar in regular grip.
1. Swing both legs forward, toes reaching for mat.
2. Body swings forward, back arching. Release grip on high bar.
3. Land on mat on balls of feet, to rear of high bar.
Finish: Extend arms out to the sides or forward. See page 151 for illustration of this dismount landing.

Start: Straight-arm support on high bar.
1. Lean body forward and extend one arm down to low bar,
   grasping it in a regular grip; retain grip with other hand.
2. Follow suit with other arm as thighs rest against high bar.
3. Straighten legs and arch back.
4. Hold; head up, arms supporting most of body weight.
Finish: Swing legs downward and push off with arms from
   low bar, ending in straight-arm support on high bar.
   Spot on shoulder and arm, as body leans forward onto low
bar, and during recovery.
Variation: Drop both arms to low bar simultaneously.

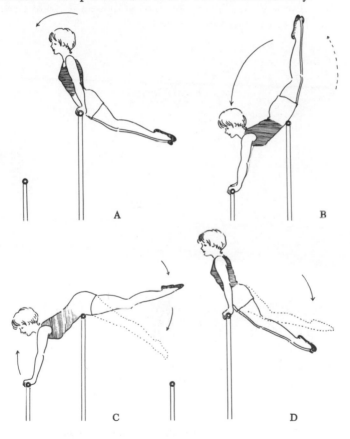

Thigh Rest

FORWARD SOMERSAULT WITH HANDSTAND DISMOUNT

Start: Swan support or straight-arm support on high bar.
1. Grip high bar with both hands in reverse grip.
2. Lean body forward and execute a somersault over high bar.
3. Touch low bar gently with legs as arms are flexed and stomach muscles control descent.
4. Bend knees and hook them around low bar.
5. Release grip on high bar and swing body down into knee hang.
6. Extend arms up over head, landing palms flat on mat.
7. Swing one leg away from low bar; staighten it; follow with other leg until both land on mat.

Forward Somersault with Handstand Dismount

Finish: Rise to stand.

Spot under high bar, on torso and legs, as necessary.

Variation: As body swings down into knee hang, grasp low
bar with both hands. Rotate body backward in backward
somersault. Rise to stand.

BACK HIP CIRCLE

Start: Straight-arm support on low bar.
1. Swing legs back forcefully and high.
2. As legs swing downward, flex hips and bring them to bar
in pike position; bend elbows.
3. Continue backward rotation until a full circle has been
completed.

Finish: Straight-arm support.

Spot forward of low bar, on hips, back, and legs, as needed.

Back Hip Circle

There are many more stunts and movements which can be performed on this apparatus. However, the basics have been covered here, and the imagination can expand these exercises into routines to be envied. A dash of showmanship adds much to any routine. This includes holding strategic, graceful and impressive poses, all performed with excellent form, plus square-cornered approach and departure from apparatus.

Advanced Stunts

SIDE CROSS HANDSTAND

Start: Crotch seat on low bar or riding seat.
1. Hand on low bar grips behind the buttocks; other hand grips high bar in regular grip.
2. Swing outer leg up, bending it at the knee, and land foot on low bar.
3. Extend other leg forward and up, knee rigid, toes pointed.
4. Lean body forward and rise on bent leg, shifting grip on low bar forward of this foot.
5. Assume forearm grip with arm on high bar.
6. Swing extended leg back and push off with the foot on low bar.
7. Kick up into handstand between the bars.
Finish: Swing down into between-bar swing—high.
    Spot above wrist and on forearm during kick-off; on forearm and back in handstand.
Variation: From handstand, hips make a quarter turn toward high bar and bend over the bar; both hands grasp high bar.
    a. Finish may be straight-arm support on high bar.
    b. Forward somersault over high bar, using reverse grip.
Variation: Slow, controlled lowering of body from handstand into crotch seat on low bar.

ARCH BACK (this is the reverse of the thigh rest).

Start: Hang on high bar, back to low bar.
1. Swing legs up; bend knees and hook them around high bar.

2. Release grip and slowly extend hands overhead.
3. Reach for low bar as body swings forward.
4. Arch back as hands grip low bar with regular grip, thumbs curling up and over bar, palms facing away from body.
5. Straighten legs, arms supporting most of body weight, back of thighs resting on top of high bar.

Finish: Bend knees, ease body down. Release grip on low bar. Return to hang. and drop to mat.

Side Cross Handstand

10

❊ ❊ ❊

BALANCE BEAM FOR GIRLS

The regulation beam has a perfectly balanced, straight surface, vital for the leaps and handstands performed in Olympic
competition. Fortunately, beam work at the elementary and
intermediate levels requires no more than a length of quality

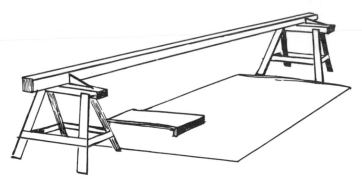

Balance Beam for Girls

hardwood, well sanded and sealed. The ideal height for the balance beam for young girls is chest height. The low beam stands about a foot off the floor. Both beams can be easily and inexpensively made and can be adjusted to the height of the performer (see the chapter on equipment).

ELEMENTARY WORK ON THE BALANCE BEAM FOR GIRLS

WALK

The first experience on the balance beam should be on a low beam or with the beam placed upon the mat. Poise and grace should be stressed from the beginning. The student should learn to look at the beam with downcast eyes and erect head and body. The walk should be practiced until walking on the beam is as easy as walking on the floor.

Start: Step up onto beam.
1. Hold body and head erect.
2. Extend arms out to the sides for balance.
3. Begin walk, placing one foot in front of the other.
4. Advance slowly, keeping the eyes on the beam.
Finish: Jump down to either side, toes leading, landing on the balls of the feet, knees bent, arms either out to the sides or extended forward.

Spot on arm or hand, as necessary to help maintain balance.

Walk

Start: Step onto beam.
1. Take one step.
2. Bring back leg forward, bend the knee and raise it, preferably until thigh is parallel to mat.
3. Slowly, with deliberate movements, advance to end of beam.
Finish: Dismount as for walk.
   Spot on arm or hand, as necessary.

Leg-Raise Walk

KNEE-DIP WALK

Start: Step onto beam; walk one step.
1. As rear leg is brought forward, leg on beam bends at knee, and advancing leg, held straight, dips below beam.

Knee-Dip Walk

2. In this fashion continue to walk to end of beam.

Finish: Jump down on either side of beam, as for walk.
 Spot on arm or hand, as necessary.

EXTENDED LEG-RAISE WALK

Start: Step onto beam; take one step forward.
1. Bring rear leg forward and raise it as high as possible
 (eventually parallel to mat). Keep knee rigid, toes pointed.
2. Repeat to end of beam, all movement slow and controlled.
Finish: Dismount as before.
 Spot on arm or hand, as necessary.

Extended Leg-Raise Walk

Turn

Start: Walk several steps along beam.
1. With one foot in front of the other, raise heels off beam, weight borne on balls of feet.
2. Pivot body 90 degrees on the balls of the feet.
3. Extend arms out to the sides to aid balance.
Finish: Lower heels onto beam, feet one in front of the other.
   Spot on the hand or arm; and at waist if necessary.

KNEEL BALANCE

Start: Stand on beam, arms out to sides.
1. Place weight on forward leg. Slowly bend forward leg.
2. As body begins to lower, bend knee of rear leg.
3. With pointed toe, slide rear leg back along beam until the knee can be placed on the beam.
4. Shift weight to knee on beam, forward leg steadying body.
5. Hold; body erect, head high, arms out to sides.
Finish: Slow rise to stand.
   Spot on arm in two places.

Kneel Balance

KNEE SCALE

Start: Kneel balance (just learned).
1. Lean body forward and grasp the beam firmly with both hands, at a point directly in front of foot—palms facing each other, thumbs on top of beam.

2. Bring forward leg slowly back and raise it as high as possible.
3. Hold; back arched, head up, extended leg straight, pointed toes.
4. Reverse movements until back to starting position.

Finish: Rise to stand, followed by dismount.

Spot on one arm in two places.

Knee Scale

KNEEL ARCH-BACK

Start: Kneel balance.
1. Lean body back slowly and extend arms upward in a "V."
2. Lean head back, arching back.
3. Hold.

Finish: Return to kneel balance and stand. Dismount.

Kneel Arch-Back

Start: Stand on beam, arms at sides.
1. Take one step forward, weight on this leg.
2. Extend arm on same side upward; the other backward; both palms down.
3. Raise other leg 3 or 4 inches from beam, toes pointed.
4. Hold; head high, back arched, arms and legs rigid.
Finish: Return to stand.
    Spot on waist if necessary.

Semi-Scale Balance

DISMOUNT

Start: Stand on beam, one leg in front of the other.
1. Bend both knees, as legs push off from beam.

Dismount

2. Jump down from beam, landing on both feet at one side of beam. Landing is on balls of feet, arms extended forward or to the sides.

Finish: Erect stand, arms at sides.

This dismount is only for use with the low beam.

JUMP DISMOUNT

Although this dismount is used primarily on the high beam or the side horse, it should be learned on the low beam.

Start: Stand on beam, one foot in front of the other.

1. Make a quarter turn on balls of feet, arms out to the sides.

Jump Dismount

2. Swing both arms high to sides while knees dip.
3. Swing both arms inward, crossing them in front of body as knees dip again.
4. With final sweep of arms out to the sides and over the head, dip knees and push off from beam with both feet.

Finish: Land on balls of feet, knees bending to cushion landing, arms out to sides for balance.

Spot in front of beam, ready to assist if needed. The high beam for girls should be even with, or slightly lower than, the base of the breastbone. This adjustment will make spotting less difficult.

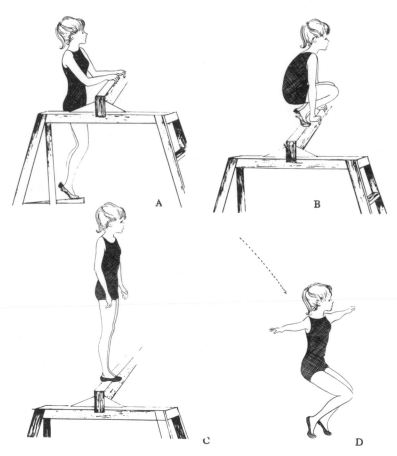

Squat Mount and Stand Dismount

Execute as the jump-off dismount on the side horse. (See figure, p. 191)

Movements on the low beam can be combined into numerous routines of various walks on the beam, plus graceful dips and bends. The fox trot, the rumba, or the cha-cha-cha can be included for added interest.

The waltz step-close-step movement combines well with the various walks and stunts already learned. The balance beam does wonders in developing poise and grace and a regal carriage. It also provides fertile ground for the imagination. The number of combinations of movements from ballroom dances and ballet are endless.

PIROUETTE

Start. Stand on beam, one leg in front of the other.
1. Place weight on rear leg.
2. Raise forward leg, toes pointed and angled inward.
3. Arch arm on same side above the head. Extend other arm gracefully out to the side, to aid balance.

Finish: Return to start position.

Spot on waist if necessary.

May be combined with waltz or other step.

Slow, gliding steps, in which the soles of the feet slide along the beam, can be added to many of the following movements.

Pirouette

Start: Forward step on beam, weight on forward leg.
1. Raise rear leg, knee rigid, toes pointed.
2. Lean body forward slightly, as leg is raised as high as possible, back arching, head up.
3. Extend one arm forward; the other back, palms down.
4. Hold.
Finish: Return to stand.
   Spot on waist.

Back-Leg Extension Balance

CROSS-HAND BALLET TOUCH

Start: Several forward steps, ending with weight on rear leg.
1. Extend front leg forward. Rear leg bends at knee or remains rigid.
2. Lean body forward as extended leg slides forward on beam.
3. Extend both arms downward, the hands crossing at farthest extent of reach.
4. Hold; extended leg rigid, toes pointed, head up.
Finish: Slow rise to stand, weight shifting to front leg.
   Spot at waist if necessary.

Variation: Extend one hand out to the side, the other as above; or extend both arms straight back, even with buttocks, palms either up or down.

Cross-Hand Ballet Touch

SUPPORTED FRONT SCALE

Start: Stand, one leg behind the other, weight on forward leg.
1. Bend body slowly forward until both hands grasp beam, thumbs on top, palms facing each other.
2. Raise rear leg high, knee rigid, toes pointed; straighten other leg.
3. Hold. Head up, back arched.
Finish: Slow rise to stand.
   Spot on one arm and extended leg.
   All movements should be learned on the low beam.

Supported Front Scale

STRAIGHT-ARM SUPPORT

This is a stunt for the high beam. Use a beatboard for the mount. It is positioned as shown on page 164. A short run-in may be used as in vaulting.
Start: Run-in or in-place double-leg takeoff.

1. Place hands on beam, flexing arms and exerting a down-ward pressure.
2. Straighten arms, bearing total body weight on them, hips resting against beam.

Finish: Return to beatboard, or lead into one of the following movements:

Straight-Arm Support

CROTCH SEAT MOUNT

Start: Sraight-arm support.

1. Arms bearing body weight, swing one leg up and over beam.

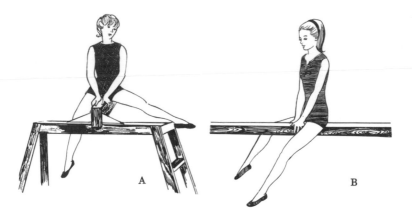

Crotch Seat Mount

2. Make a quarter turn of body as weight shifts to buttocks and the inner thighs.
3. Regrip, thumbs on top of beam, palms facing each other. Grip may be in front of or behind the body.

Finish: Retrace movements and return to beatboard, or lead into V-seat.

Spot on mount side of beam on the upper arm and forearm.
This move leads into stunts performed in a sit position.

V-SEAT

Start: Crotch-seat mount.
1. Place both hands behind the buttocks.
2. Both legs, held straight with pointed toes, swing up and rest on the beam.
3. Hold; head high, back arched.
4. Lean body backward, bending elbows.
5. Slowly raise legs as high as possible.
6. Hold several seconds; legs rigid, toes pointed.

Finish: Lower legs slowly; return to crotch seat.

Spot on upper arm and small of back.
This exercise should be well mastered as it is of great value to girls of all ages. It can be practiced on the low beam.

V-Seat

SUPINE ARCH-UP

Start: Sit on beam in crotch position.
1. With both hands, grasp beam, behind the buttocks.
2. Raise legs and place them on beam, legs straight, toes pointed.

3. Slowly raise body off the beam, back arching, head leaned back.
4. Weight becomes evenly distributed between arms and feet.
5. Hold; legs straight.

Finish: Return to sit position.

Spot on upper arm and forearm. It may be helpful, at first, to spot on the upper arm and small of back, this arm passing under the back, the hand holding the waist.

Variation: While in full position, bend one leg at the knee and slowly slide it up the beam.

Supine Arch-Up

FORWARD SPINE STRETCH

Start: Sit on beam, legs extended forward along beam, arms behind buttocks.
1. Slide hands forward along side of beam as body bends forward.
2. Grasp beam firmly at extreme end of reach.
3. Bend body forward and down as far as comfort allows. Straining should be avoided.
4. Hold; legs straight, toes pointed, head bent down.

Finish: Return to sit.

Spot at the waist if necessary.

Time and practice stretch the spine and rear leg muscles painlessly.

Forward Spine Stretch

178

Start: Straddle sit on beam, hands behind buttocks.

1. Swing legs up and place them on beam. Stretch one leg out; bend the other.
2. Hands behind buttocks, lean body back into lying position.
3. Extend arms above the head, grasp beam, behind the head, fingers curled beneath beam, palms facing each other on either side of beam.
4. Spread legs and lower them below level of beam; arch back.
5. Hold momentarily; legs straight, toes pointed.
6. Slowly bring legs together and raise them until perpendicular to beam.
7. Hold.

Finish: Slow return to lying position on beam; then to sit. Spot on waist and legs.

Variation: As legs are extended upward, bend one leg and rest sole of this foot on knee of other leg; *or* spread legs into "V."

At this point the student should be quite at ease on the beam. Little girls often reach a plateau and do not advance

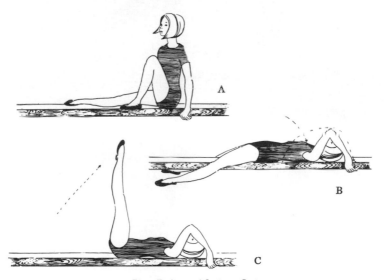

Leg Raise with Lay-Out

beyond it for some time. Whether they become really proficient is not the chief consideration; the purpose of all phases of apparatus work is enjoyment, fitness, and the habit of vigorous physical activity. Holding to rigid standards of progress in apparatus work does not achieve these goals.

INTERMEDIATE WORK

BACKWARD KICK DISMOUNT

Start: Crotch seat, hands in front of thighs.
1. Swing legs back until one foot can be placed on beam.
2. Weight is now equally borne by arms and instep (or toes if easier) of one foot.
3. With other leg, practice swinging forward, then up and back, until it clears about 5 inches above the beam.
4. At height of a backward swing, momentum lifts foot on beam. Raise both legs above beam and swing off to either side. Land on same side as swinging foot.

Backward Kick Dismount

5. Use arms to help guide body to chosen side, then push off.

Finish: Land on mat, hand nearest beam retaining its grip. Spot on arms and legs, if necessary.

Variation: From crotch-seat, kick both legs back simultaneously. Land on either side of beam.

   If a beatboard is used, landing is always on the opposite side.

Variation: In time, both legs can kick up high and meet in a semi-handstand; body parallel to beam, feet level with head.

STRADDLE MOUNT

Start: Run-in takeoff from beatboard.

1. Hands flat on beam, begin to spread legs to sides immediately after they leave beatboard. Keep knees rigid.
2. With legs spread, land feet out to either side of hands.
3. Straighten back, head arching up, legs rigid.
4. Hold.

Finish: Dismount back to beatboard. Legs may be bent at knees and brought closer to hands before leaving beam. Spot forward of beam, on arm and shoulder.

Variation: Extend one leg out to side. Bend the other and land it on beam between the hands.

Variation: Same as above, except that extended leg is raised parallel to beam. (This is the wolf-vault mount.)

Straddle Mount

Start: Straddle mount.
1. Transfer weight to arms as hips are lowered slowly to beam.
2. Rest hips on beam, head arched, back erect.
3. Slowly lift hips and legs off beam.
4. Hold.
Finish: Return hips to beam; assume crotch seat or chosen position.
   Spot on upper arm and back.
Variation: Legs may be brought closer together for hold.

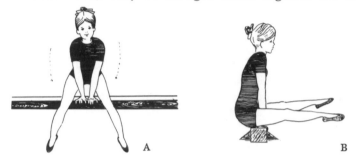

A   B

Straddle Hold

SHOULDER STAND

Start: Sit on beam, legs extended forward along beam.
1. Bend one leg and grasp beam behind buttocks.
2. Slowly lower body into a lay-out.
3. Regrip beam above the head, fingers curling under beam, palms facing each other.
4. Spread legs and lower them on either side of beam. Arch the back and bend head back on one side of beam.
5. Slowly raise legs and bring them together. Gradually elevate the torso until legs are parallel to beam.
6. Slowly, and with full control, straighten body.
7. Hold.
Finish: Lower body into pike position, legs parallel to beam, then into start position.
Spot at waist during ascent; on hips in full position.

Variation: To simplify, instead of rising into shoulder stand, continue backward rotation of legs until toes touch beam behind head. Return to lay-out, *or* extend only one leg upward. The other remains parallel to beam.

The shoulder stand should be mastered first on a mat; then the performer is ready to transfer this movement to the low or high beams.

As the full shoulder stand is held, one shoulder bears full body weight. A bruise may develop on the shoulder at first. This may be caused by improper positioning of the shoulder on the beam. Muscle, not bone, should touch the apparatus.

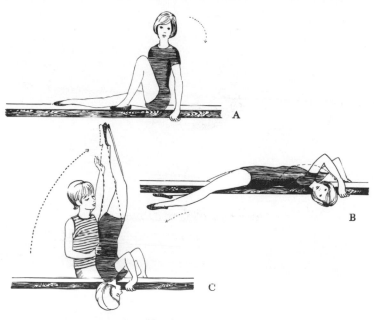

Shoulder Stand

SCALE

Start: Stand on beam.
1. Place weight on one leg, lean body forward, and raise other leg as high as possible.
2. Extend arms out to sides.
3. Hold head up, arch back.

Finish: Start position; or lead into another movement.
    Spot on leg and arm, if necessary.
Variation: Bend elevated leg at knee and grasp instep with one hand. Extend other arm forward, palm down.
Variation: From scale, bend body down. Grasp with both hands the beam in front of foot, forehead touching shin. Raise extended leg as high as possible, ideal position being legs in a straight, vertical line. This is a needle scale.

At this point, girls can compile a good routine by adding movements of their own invention. The balance beam is the fun way to perfect posture and poise.

Scale

11

❀ ❀ ❀

SIDE HORSE VAULTING

Essentially the horse is a padded obstacle over which a variety of vaults can be executed. It should be approached from the side, as shown in the illustration which appears on page 186. Side-horse activity is much enjoyed by children because it fulfills the desire to climb on or over anything in sight.

Although the regulation side horse is too high for small children, they, too, can enjoy this activity when a springboard is used on the approach side. A beatboard or a low springboard should be used by older children. A beatboard is an inclined plane with a nonslip surface. It is also a basic piece of apparatus for children's indoor broadjump. (See figures p. 205)

It is wise to secure a side horse which has pommels (handles) rather than a long horse, which has none, since the side horse may be used for several more advanced movements. If a standard side horse or long horse is not available, a balance beam with a small mat wrapped around it and secured at each end by a rope or strap will do nicely for the small children. The springboard makes the standard horse available to small children for vaulting activities. (See figure p. 56)

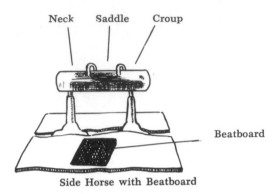

Side Horse with Beatboard

RUNNING APPROACH TO HORSE

Start: Run-in of several yards.
1. Time approach to end in two or three steps on the beatboard and one double-leg jump takeoff near edge of board.
2. Execute takeoff in place, at point of last step.
3. Grasp pommels, with palms facing inward, thumbs curled around inner side of pommels. If a buck, or long horse, is used, land hands flat on padded surface.
4. As legs push off from beatboard, flex arms and press down.
Finish: Mount horse in straight-arm support.

Spot on upper arm and above wrist, spotter on front of horse, to one side of performer.

A   B   C

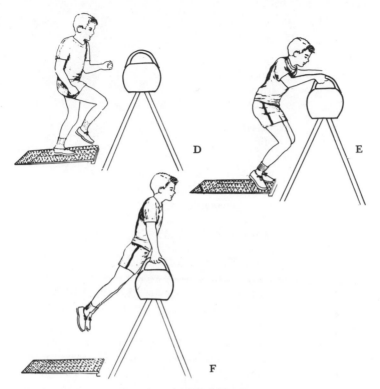

D

E

F

Running Approach to Horse

K N E E - R E S T   M O U N T

Start: Double-leg takeoff from beatboard, hands on pommels
  or flat on padded surface.
1. As feet push off, flex arms and push down. Bend legs up
  into kneel position on horse, toes pointed.
2. Release hands from pommels and extend backward at
  sides.
3. Straighten torso, head held erect.
4. Hold several seconds.
Finish: Regrasp pommels, or return to flat horse as legs return
  to beatboard; support body weight with arms until in
  stand.
  Spot on upper arm and above wrist, spotter in front of horse
and to side of performer.

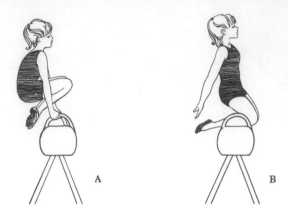

Knee-Rest Mount

BACK-REST MOUNT

Start: Double-leg takeoff, as just learned.
1. Bend legs; land on horse in knee rest.
2. Arms supporting body, pass legs over horse; straighten and point forward and down, knees rigid, toes pointed.
3. Hold; back erect, head up.
4. Extend legs forward as performer drops from horse.
Finish: Land on mat, toes leading, balls of feet bearing body weight. Bend knees to cushion shock.

Spot on upper arm and forearm above wrist. Spotter is positioned in front of horse and to side of performer.

Back-Rest Mount

Start: Back-rest mount.
1. Whip legs backward, then swing forward forcefully.
2. Push off from horse with arms, legs straight, toes pointed.
3. Release grasp on pommels.
4. Land on balls of feet, bending knees to absorb shock.
Finish: Stand at attention.

Spot as before for backward rest mount.

This dismount should be well learned, as it is the basis for a safe, sure landing in all succeeding vaults.

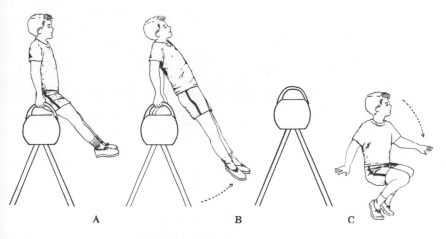

A   B   C

Back-Rest Dismount

SQUAT VAULT

Start: Short run-in, double-leg takeoff, hands on pommels.
1. Bend legs and land feet on horse, body in squat.
2. Hold; head raised and back erect.
3. Transfer weight to arms as legs thrust forward and straighten, arms pushing off from horse.
4. Reach for mat with pointed toes.
Finish: Land on balls of feet, knees bending.

After some practice, the hold is eliminated, making the action a smooth uninterrupted vault.

Spot in front of horse, grasping arm in two places.

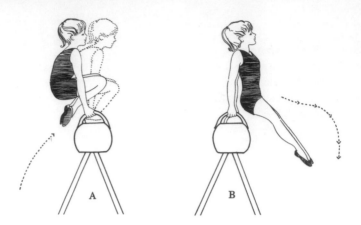

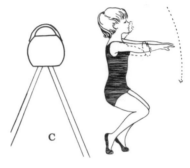

Squat Vault

JUMP-OFF DISMOUNT

Start: Jump to squat.

1. Release grip on pommels and rise into stand position, body erect, head up.
2. Hold several seconds.
3. Raise arms to front, palms down.
4. Bend knees and push off with legs. Swing arms up, followed by jump-off to mat.
5. Toes leading, land on balls of feet, bending knees to cushion jump.

Finish: Both arms extend to sides as knees bend; erect stand.

Spot in front of horse and to side of performer, ready to assist if necessary.

Jump-Off Dismount

STRADDLE REST

Start. Run in or stationary double-leg takeoff.

1. Bend one leg and pass it between the arms. Place leg over the horse, arms bearing body weight.
2. Hold both legs rigid, toes pointing, body erect, head held high.
3. Hold several seconds.
4. Bend rear leg and pass it between the arms, coming to rest next to other leg. Both legs are straight, toes pointed.
5. Execute back-rest dismount.

Finish: Make neat landing on mat.

Spot on arm in two places, as previously described.

Variation: Swing back leg up and over the horse from the side, turning body a quarter turn as the hand, now between the legs, releases grip and feet land on mat. Other hand retains grip on pommel or padded surface.

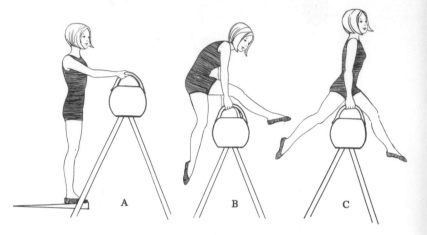

Straddle Rest

BACK REST FROM STRADDLE REST

Start: Straddle rest.
1. Swing rear leg up and over from the side, knee rigid, toes pointed.
2. As leg clears horse, bear body weight on opposite arm.
3. Release grip momentarily while leg swings over the pommel.
4. Leg having cleared pommel, regrip hand as legs come together in front of horse.

Finish: Back rest followed by back-rest dismount.
Variation: Execute stunt with other leg; with both legs, in series.

Spot on the arm in two places, standing on side which will bear body weight during stunt.

NOTE: If there is some difficulty at first, the leg may be rested momentarily on the horse while grip is changed, as illustrated on page 193.

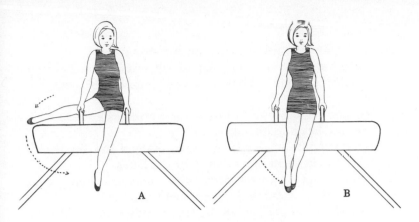

Back Rest from Straddle Rest

LEG EXTENSION VAULT

Start: Run-in and double-leg takeoff from beatboard.

1. Pass one leg between the arms, knee bent.
2. Extend other leg out to the side, head held high.
3. As body passes over horse, push off with arms.

Finish: Land on mat, arms extended out to sides or forward, to aid in maintaining balance.

    Spot, in front of horse, on forearm and upper arm.

Variation: Slant bent leg to side and pass it over the horse in a horizontal position.

    Care must be taken during the learning stages to prevent a head-first landing. Stressing the erect head is helpful.

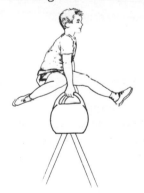

Leg Extension Vault

Start: Run-in of several yards, double-leg takeoff.

1. Spread straightened legs out to sides. Land on horse in straddle position, hands grasping pommels between the legs.
2. Release grip and jump to the mat, arms extended in "V" over the head and out to sides.
3. Once straddle mount is mastered, extend the legs (after takeoff) out to the sides and clear the horse.
4. Push off vigorously with arms from pommels as body passes over horse in straddle position, head held up.
5. As body nears mat, bring the legs together in a neat landing on balls of feet, knees bending to cushion shock.

Finish: As knees bend, extend arms out to sides.

Spot on front shoulder; arm and shoulder for landing. Retain grip until dismount is complete.

Straddle Vault

PENDULUM SWING

Start: Straight-arm support.

1. Grip pommels with hands and swing both legs from side to side. Keep knees rigid, toes pointed.
2. Swing will be low at first as weight shifts from one arm to the other.
3. Stop all motion.

Finish: Drop to beatboard.

194

Spot, if confidence is needed, by grasping waist from behind to assist in the swing and to offset a weakening of the arms. (Generally not necessary.)

This is preparation for side-horse-support exercise in men's gymnastics. Girls need not work as hard on this as boys.

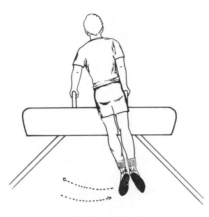

Pendulum Swing

STRADDLE-SEAT VAULT AND DISMOUNT

Start: Short run-in, or in-place double-leg takeoff.

1. Swing one leg to side and up and over the horse.
2. Make quarter turn of body, followed by a straddle sit on horse.
3. Move both hands to pommel nearest the body.
4. Kick back other leg forcefully, clearing the horse.
5. Bear body weight on both arms; legs rigid, toes pointed.
6. Execute another quarter turn as legs come together and land on mat, body facing horse.

Finish: Retain grip with one hand, extend other arm to side to assist in balance, and for a polished finish.

Spot on arm in two places, spotter positioned in front of horse, between pommels, stepping back as landing is executed.

Variation: Both legs swing back, then forward of horse, from straddle-sit position. Flex hips and both legs land on mat, omitting the quarter turn.

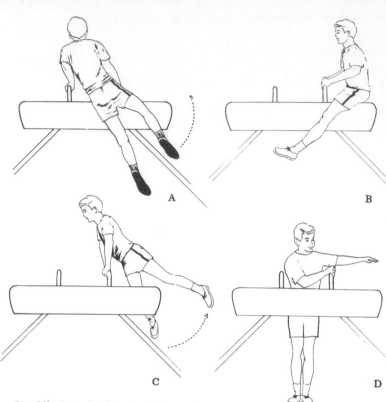

Straddle-Seat Vault and Dismount

STRADDLE MOUNT AND HALF-CIRCLE DISMOUNT

Start: Jump to straddle mount.

1. Grip pommels with both hands; legs straight, head up.
2. Shift weight to arms as legs leave horse, freeing body to execute a quarter turn, hips held high.
3. Continue movement over the horse, until both legs clear the horse.
4. Bring legs together as arm closest to body releases grip and legs land on mat.

Finish: Retain grip on pommel with one hand and extend the other to the side.

Spot on both arms, spotter stepping back for landing.

To make learning easier, legs may come to a momentary

196

rest on the horse at the end of the first quarter turn.

Variation: To simplify, the knees may be slightly bent throughout the half-turn.

These movements should give the student a good background in basic vaulting skills. The following stunt may be
introduced when the teacher feels it can be mastered readily.

It strengthens both the upper leg and abdominal muscles and
is suitable for both boys and girls.

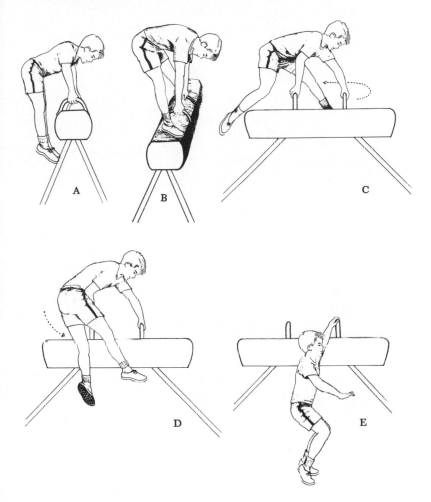

Straddle Mount and Half-Circle Dismount

Start: Front-rest position (straight-arm support).

1. Swing first one leg, then the other, over the horse, releasing hands momentarily to allow legs to pass in front of horse.
2. Assume back-rest position.
3. Place buttocks on horse and slowly elevate legs until they are parallel to mat.
4. Hold.
5. Lower legs slowly and return to back rest.

Finish: Back-rest dismount with quarter turn.

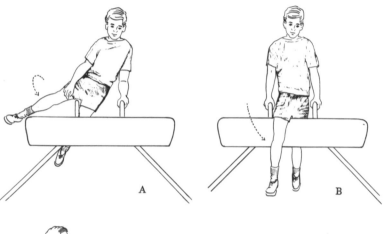

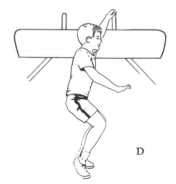

Straddle Mount from Side to Front-Rest Lever

Variation: Bear body weight on arms while legs are raised. Hold.

Children have a tendency to skip the fundamental slow moves which should precede the vault. The patient learner soon becomes a polished performer; he is also the one who needs the least assistance. Young children progress slowly, frequently being satisfied with the first few vaults shown. The play element is the primary interest. Those who show ambition should, of course, be encouraged to go further. Should a vault prove difficult, it should be eliminated until more skill has been acquired.

INTERMEDIATE SIDE HORSE VAULTING

HANDSPRING OVER HORSE

Start: Run-in with double-leg takeoff from beatboard.
   (Pommels are removed from the side horse; long horse or mat-wrapped balance beam adjusted at approximately chest level.)
1. Make good takeoff from beatboard with both legs.
2. Land hands flat on horse.

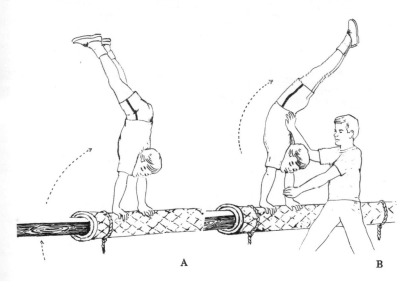

A   B

Handspring over Horse

3. Thrust both legs up and over, as back begins to arch. Hold head up.
4. As legs continue over, extend them to mat.

Finish: Land on both feet, extending arms out to the sides.

Spot forward and to side of horse. Grip is on forearm and shoulder as body assumes handstand position; on forearm and behind the shoulders for descent to mat and landing. Should the shoulders fail to rotate upward, the hand behind the shoulders lifts them and prevents a head-first landing.

If the horse cannot be lowered sufficiently, use a small springboard. It is a good idea to pad the landing area with several mats.

Variation: Execute a quarter turn prior to landing.

Exercises executed in a straight-arm support, called side-horse-support exercises, are not covered here. They require powerful arms and shoulders and are beyond the physical capabilities of elementary and junior high school boys. Girls and women never engage in side-horse-support work.

12

❀ ❀ ❀

ROPE CLIMB

Rope climb is an inexpensive and popular indoor-outdoor activity which builds the often neglected arms and upper torso. The 1-inch manila rope should have a large knot about 1 foot from its end (which just touches the ground) and should be given a periodic safety check.

ROPE CLIMB

Start: Stand at foot of rope, spotter holding rope at base.
1. Grasp rope with one hand above the other, palms on outside, thumbs curled around opposite side of rope.
2. Flex arms and pull body up, simultaneously drawing knees up and circling rope tightly with feet.
3. Straighten knees, lifting body.
4. Move hands up along rope until arms are nearly straight. Bend elbows as arms pull up.
Finish: As high ascents as possible without much tiring, followed by *hand-over-hand* descent. Do not slide hands along rope. It can result in nasty rope burns.
Spot by boosting body at waist, if needed. Spotter stands at

foot of rope, ready to assist, as needed, and steps on rope with one foot to render it taut.

When rope is attached to playground swing equipment, the ground beneath the point of suspension should be dug out to a depth of 6 inches and replaced with sand. Rope may be attached, lasso style, to supporting bar of swing equipment and removed when rope is not in use.

Rope Climb

ROPE CLIMB FOR OLDER BOYS

Start: Sit on mat below rope, legs outspread around rope base.
1. Grasp rope, hands one above the other.
2. Hand-over-hand, pull the body up, using only the arms. Legs remain rigid and extended outward.
Finish: Hand-over-hand descent to mat, landing in start position.

13

❀ ❀ ❀

TRACK EVENTS

High Jump

Children enjoy the high jump. The equipment needed is inexpensive. A *bamboo rod* is used in the high jump for children. It is lightweight and bounces away easily when hit, thereby preventing injuries. It is vital that the rod be placed on the side *toward* which the children jump so that it will bounce out and away from the jumper. For small children, standards may have to be modified as illustrated on page 60. For children in the lower elementary grades, mats should be placed in front of and behind the high-jump rod to prevent the performer from slipping, just before the apparatus is reached.

Refer to the chapter on spotting for "Spotting Track Events."

SCISSORS FORM

Start: Run-in at a 40-degree angle to rod.
1. Retain approach angle and swing up leg nearest rod.
2. Push off with leg on mat.
3. Swing leading leg up and over rod, trailing leg following.
Finish: Land on leading leg.

Scissors Form

A scissors jump is used to obtain good height. Each individual will discover by trial from which direction he jumps best. Some people are left-footed jumpers, others right-footed. Note that the rod is on the side *toward* which the student jumps, otherwise the rod would not fall when hit, thereby causing the standards to be toppled or resulting in injury. Use a double mat on the landing side. For the very young, place a mat on the approach side.

STRADDLE FORM

(This is for older children, mainly boys.)
Start: Run-in approach at an angle to rod.
1. Place leading leg in front of rod at a 90-degree angle to rod.
2. Begin upward and over thrust of other leg, parallel to rod.
3. Turn body toward the bar as takeoff foot pushes off forcefully from floor.
4. Head, chest, and shoulders extended upward. Swing arms up over rod.
5. Rotate takeoff leg, toes turned upward, as body passes over and parallel to rod.
Finish: Let one hand and foot touch padding first, absorbing landing shock; follow with other leg and shoulder. Recover into a stand.

It is vital that at least two mats be placed on landing side of rod. Sneakers should be worn.

Straddle Form

The Beatboard

The regulation beatboard is a simple structure used as a takeoff board for the broad jump, the high balance beam, the side horse, or the uneven parallel bars. It can be easily constructed of wood. A runner of ribbed rubber or plastic nailed or glued to the beatboard will form a nonslip surface. Strips of rubber glued to bottom surfaces will prevent the beatboard from slipping, and the lower edges of the beatboard should be planed for stability. Some beatboards have a slight spring action. A simple beatboard can be easily and inexpensively made.

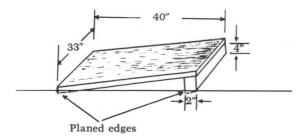

Beatboard

Broad Jump

INDOOR BROAD JUMP

This type of broad jump is enjoyed by the younger children who have neither the patience nor the endurance for standard broad jump. Do not expect them to achieve any great distance.
Start: Stand at edge of beatboard, feet together.
1. Swing arms forward, bending knees.
2. Swing arms back, bending knees.
3. Swing arms forward forcefully, as knees bend and both feet push off hard.
Finish: Land on both feet on measurement runner.

Though no spotting is necessary, it is important that some person keep score and readjust the equipment as needed, in order that the activity be meaningful to the children. Mats should be placed under the beatboard and the measurement runner.

The measurement runner is made of ribbed rubber or plastic and is marked with measurements.

Mat

Broad Jump

OUTDOOR BROAD JUMP

In this type of broad jump the run-in is all important. It is the speed of the run-in which makes a good long-distance jump.
Start: Feet together about 24 paces from takeoff board.
1. Break into full-speed run. At 3 steps from board, decrease speed slightly in order to crouch.
2. Hit board hard and take off on the jump.
Finish: Land on well-padded area and observe measure.

206

The sand in the landing pit must be leveled after each jump, so that adequate padding is always present.

Many children who find other activities difficult find relay racing a highly satisfying activity. Relay races can be practiced on a smooth lawn or other area which offers a good surface for running; or indoors, if the gym is large.

A good method for relays is that used by Clyde Littlefield: A bamboo baton is passed from runner to runner at hip level, being grasped palm down. The receiver extends his arm back and forms a "V" between the thumb and fingers to grasp and pass the baton. From three to five children comprise each team. In competition, it is wise to alternate the fast and slower runners, saving the fastest runner for last.

LOW HURDLES

Start: Crouch position some distance from the first hurdle.
 (The distance between hurdles depends on size of children and facility. It should allow for a reasonable run-in.)
1. Run-in to first hurdle.
2. Lean body forward, extending leading leg straight forward, thus beginning first stride over hurdle.
3. Having cleared hurdle, bring leg down sharply.
4. Keep rear leg on ground as long as possible, then bring it up and off to the side in a bent position.

The hurdles should be taken in the middle of a long stride. Jumping is to be avoided. When hurdling over the low hurdles, the leading leg may be bent and the rear leg brought forward more quickly. As skill improves, the level of the hurdles can be raised.

When hurdling is done indoors, mats should be placed along the entire path and behind each hurdle. For younger children, a bamboo pole may be used in place of the hurdle beam. It is light and will not cause injury. The hurdles should be set up so the curved end faces in the direction in which the hurdles are being run. If facing the opposite direction they will not topple.

A

B

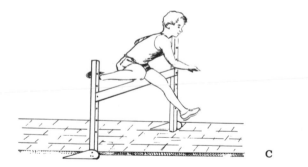

C

Low Hurdles

14

❋ ❋ ❋

GAMES FOR YOUNGER CHILDREN

Everyone enjoys the fun of a game but selecting the right games for younger boys and girls can be something of a problem. They have outgrown the "Around the Mulberry Bush" type of activity and are not yet mature enough to participate in regulation volleyball and similar group games.

By bending the rules to simplify certain games, the instructor can bring to small children the enjoyment and benefits of game playing.

Included in this chapter are some of the old-time favorites which, for some reason, seem to have faded into obscurity. Since inexpensive items are the only equipment needed, these games can blend into almost any program. Indoors or in the playground they fill in those last five or ten minutes which remain after the more organized activities are completed. The rules are so flexible that an abrupt ending to the game does not in any way interfere with its enjoyment.

Following these examples, the rules of other games can be altered, thereby rounding out any physical training program so that it offers both the self-competition of the more dynamic sports and the team efforts which teach good fellowship and cooperation.

GROUP ROPE JUMP

The children form a circle. The instructor stands in the center. A long manila rope, about 1 inch in diameter with a sand-filled sock or knot tied at one end, is then rotated by the instructor at a moderate speed around the circle. Each child jumps up as the rope goes by to avoid letting it touch him. Anyone touched by the rope is eliminated from the game. As the game progresses, the rope may be rotated faster and faster to add excitement to the game. This game may be played either indoors or outdoors. Note that the sand-filled sock or the knot in the rope is outside the circle and cannot hit the legs of the children.

A

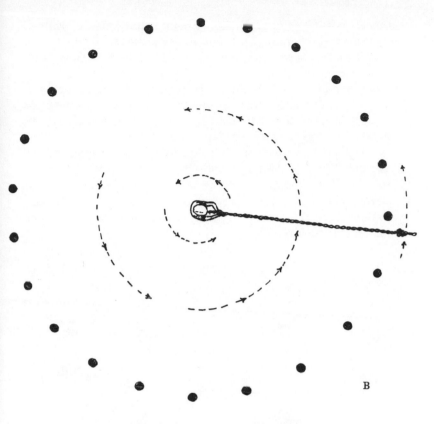

B

Group Rope Jump

CRAB VOLLEYBALL

Played with a plastic ball of volleyball size, this version of volleyball is played in the "crab" position. This position is assumed by sitting on the floor, knees bent and arms extended to the back, palms placed so that it is comfortable for the child to raise the buttocks from the floor and support himself on his hands while moving about.

A line on the gym floor, or a rope stretched some distance, is used to separate the two teams. Any reasonable number of children may comprise a team. The ball is then thrown to the starting team, and the players attempt to make the opposite team members either miss kicking the ball or kick it so that it goes out of bounds. Out-of-bounds lines are determined by some type of marker, depending upon the size of the teams. Chalk marks, ropes, etc., will do nicely. This is a good body-toning activity.

Rules can be very flexible, the point of the game being to keep the ball from going out of bounds or from touching the floor with more than one bounce. It is not permissible for the hands or arms to touch the ball, and the ball must be kicked by the feet. Circumstances will dictate the most practical set of rules. When playing outdoors, for example, it is impractical to allow for a bounce because balls do not bounce well on lawns. Also, for skillful players indoors, the instructor may wish to allow no bounce. It is not advisable to play this game on a concrete surface.

Crab Volleyball

KICK BALL

This is but one version of kick ball. The game is based on the positions and playing-field markings of baseball, as are the basic rotation and line-up of teams. However, both team numbers and the size of the playing diamond are flexible.

The pitcher *rolls* a large ball (volleyball size) to the kicker positioned at home base. The kicker tries to kick the ball so as to prevent its catch by the opposing team, so he can run around the bases and back to home base. The ball may be rolled or thrown by the opposing team to enable their team-mates to touch or tag the runner with the ball, thus making the runner "out." If a lightweight plastic ball is used, the runner may be eliminated by throwing the ball at him.

Kick ball is basically baseball, except that the ball is kicked rather than batted and rolled to the kicker rather than thrown. Members of the team up to kick wait on the side, as in base-ball, while the opposing team is positioned on the diamond on the other three bases and in the area beyond, as deemed neces-sary. The catcher can be from either team.

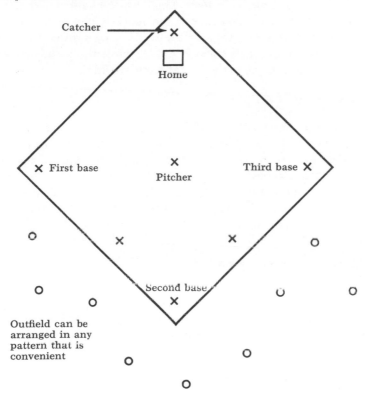

For the younger child it is best to move the position of the pitcher closer to home plate

Kick Ball

A point is scored whenever the kicker completes a full tour of the bases. The runner may go around a second or third time, which is a frequent occurrence with a good long-distance kick. Each complete circle of the bases counts for one point. In this way, one kicker may make as many as three points on one kick. This game can also be played in the gym, using small sandbags for bases.

Relay Games

HOP RELAY

Class is split into two or three teams. A marker of some sort, pole, sandbag, chalk marks on gym floor, etc., is placed at some distance from each team. One at a time a member from each team hops on one foot to the marker, circles behind it and returns at a run, tagging the waiting team member. The tagged teammate then starts hopping, while the member who just finished returns to the end of his team line.

DRIBBLE RELAY

Using the same rules as above, a basketball or a volleyball is dribbled to the marker and back. For added interest, the marker may be a basketball basket, in which case a basket must be made before the child may return to the line. He returns either at a run or still dribbling the ball, hands the ball to the next child in line, then returns to the end of the line. This is excellent for developing coordination.

SOMERSAULT RELAY

Each team is lined up before a tumbling mat or on a good lawn area. One at a time, members from each team somersault to the end of the mat, or to a spot marked on the grass, run back, tag the next child in line, and return to the end of the line.

LEAP-FROG RELAY

Same as above, except that two members participate in the stunt, across the mat.

214

Starting out in the position assumed for push-ups, team members "walk" in this position across the mat or lawn area, return, and tag the next child in line. This is excellent for the upper torso.

JUMP ROPE RELAY

The children skip rope to the marker. Should a team member fail to make the required distance without error, he must return to starting point and begin again. Other rules are the same as for somersault relay.

HIP-WALK RELAY

Seated on the mat or lawn, facing the marker, the child thrusts one fully extended leg forward, lifting the buttock on that side and moving it forward. This is repeated with the other leg and hip and results in a sort of hip-waddle. The arms are crossed and extended in this position in front of the chest. He returns at a run to tag the next child in line.

INDIAN CLUB RELAY

In relay fashion, each team runs to a stand of Indian clubs (one for each member of the team) and returns to the end of the line. When the last member has a club, the reverse is repeated until all clubs are again in one group as before. (Empty plastic bleach bottles, medium-size, partly filled with sand, tops screwed on, make an excellent substitute for Indian clubs. They are easy to grasp because of the handle, and their weight can be regulated by adding or spilling out sand.)

MODIFIED VOLLEYBALL

The class is split into two teams. The net should be lowered for young children and a lightweight plastic ball used. One side serves with any of the time-tested volleyball serves. The only rule is to keep the ball from touching the ground and keep it volleying back and forth over the net. To simplify the game only an out-of-bounds shot or a touch to the ground or floor constitutes a point for the opposing side. In lieu of a net, a rope may be streached between two posts, or trees. In this way, first, second, and third graders can be introduced to the fun of volleyball. Throwing may be substituted for volleying.

MODIFIED SOCCER

The class is lined up in two even lines facing each other at a distance of about 40 feet. A plastic ball, volleyball size, is then kicked from one side to the other, in an effort to keep the ball from getting through the line or going off to the side. Again, either a breakthrough or a foul constitutes a point for the opposing team.

TUG-O-WAR

The old familiar picnic pastime is an excellent body builder. A long piece of 1-inch manila rope is the only equipment needed. Children are split into two equal teams, taking into consideration size and weight. The teams each line up along the rope, grasp it firmly, beginning some distance from the center. A line is made through the center between the two teams. The teams begin to pull with all their strength. The team that pulls the greatest number of members of the opposing team over that line is the victor. But victor or loser, everyone wins, for all have achieved the goal of the gymnastic program—fitness through fun.

INDEX